Make Your Own Living Trust & Avoid Probate

EstateBee

By EstateBee Publishing

Bibliographic Data

- International Standard Book Number (ISBN)): 978-1-913889-13-5
- Printed in the United States of America
- First Edition: April 2008
- Second Edition: March 2014
- Third Edition: November 2020

Published By:
EstateBee Limited,
23 Lynn Road,
London SW12 9LB
United Kingdom

Printed and Distributed By: Kindle Direct Publishing, an Amazon Company

For more information, e-mail books@estate-bee.com.

Important Note

This book is meant as a general guide to preparing your own revocable living trust. While effort has been made to make this book as accurate as possible, laws and their interpretation are constantly changing. As such, you are advised to update this information with your own research and/or counsel and to consult with your personal legal, financial, and/or medical advisors before acting on any information contained in this book.

The purpose of this book is to educate and entertain. It is not meant to provide legal, financial, or medical advice or to create any attorney-client or other advisory relationship. The authors and publisher shall have neither liability (whether in negligence or otherwise) nor responsibility to any person or entity with respect to any loss or damage caused or alleged to be caused directly or indirectly by the information contained in this book or the use of that information.

About EstateBee

EstateBee, the international self-help legal publisher, was founded in 2000 by lawyers from one of the most prestigious international law firms in the World.

Our aim was simple - to provide access to quality legal information and products at an affordable price.

Our will writing software was first published in that year and, following its adaptation to cater for the legal systems of various countries worldwide, quickly drew more than 40,000 visitors per month to our website. From this humble start, EstateBee has quickly grown to become a leading international estate planning and asset protection self-help publisher with legal titles in the United States, Canada, the United Kingdom, Australia, and Ireland.

Our publications provide customers with the confidence and knowledge to help them deal with everyday estate planning issues such as the preparation of a last will and testament, a living trust, a power of attorney, administering an estate and much more.

By providing customers with much needed information and forms, we enable them to place themselves in a position where they can protect both themselves and their families using easy to read legal documents and forward planning techniques.

The Future....

We are always seeking to expand and improve the products and services we offer. However, to do this, we need to hear from interested authors and to receive feedback from our customers.

If something is not clear to you in one of our publications, please let us know and we will try to make it clearer in the next edition. If you cannot find the answer you want and have a suggestion for an addition to our range, we will happily look at that too.

Using Self-Help Books

Before using a self-help book, you need to carefully consider the advantages and disadvantages of doing so – particularly where the subject matter is of a legal or tax related nature.

In writing our self-help books, we try to provide readers with an overview of the laws in a specific area, as well as some sample documents. While this overview is often general in nature, it provides a good starting point for those wishing to carry out a more detailed review of a topic.

However, unlike an attorney advising a client, we cannot cover every conceivable eventuality that might affect our readers. Within the intended scope of this book, we can only cover the principal areas in each topic, and even where we cover these areas, we can still only do so to a moderate extent. To do otherwise would result in the writing of a textbook which would be capable of use by legal professionals. This is not what we do.

We try to present useful information and documents that can be used by an average reader with little or no legal knowledge. While our sample documents can be used in most cases, everybody's personal circumstances are different. As such, they may not be suitable for everyone. You may have personal circumstances which might impact the effectiveness of these documents or even your desire to use them. The reality is that without engaging an attorney to review your personal circumstances, this risk will always exist. It's for this very reason that you need to consider whether the cost of using a do-it-yourself legal document outweighs the risk that there may be something special about your particular circumstances which might not be taken into account by the sample documents attached to this book (or indeed any other sample documents).

It goes without saying (we hope) that if you are in any doubt as to whether the documents in this book are suitable for use in your particular circumstances, you should contact a suitably qualified attorney for advice before using them. Remember the decision to use these documents is yours. We are not advising you in any respect.

In using this book, you should also consider the fact that this book has been written with the purpose of providing a general overview of the laws in the United States. As such, it does not attempt to cover all the various procedural nuances and specific requirements that may apply from state to state – although we do point some of these out along the way. Rather, in our book, we try to provide forms which give a fair example of the type of forms which are commonly used in most states. Nevertheless, it remains possible that your state may have specific requirements which have not been taken into account in our forms.

Another thing that you should remember is that the law changes – thousands of new laws are brought into force every day and, by the same token, thousands are repealed or amended every day. As such, it is possible that while you are reading this book, the law might well have been changed. We hope it has not, but the chance does exist. To address this, when we become aware of them, we do send updates to our customers about material changes to the law. We also ensure that our books are reviewed and revised regularly to take account of these changes.

Anyway, assuming that all the above is acceptable to you, let us move on to exploring the topic at hand.........living trusts.

Table of Contents

CHAPTER 3
An Introduction to Trusts 37

CHAPTER 4
Advantages and Disadvantages of Living Trusts. 45

CHAPTER 5
Types of Living Trusts 59

CHAPTER 6
Trustees & Successor Trustees 71

CHAPTER 7
Making Gifts Under Your Living Trust 85

CHAPTER 8
Estate Taxes. 101

CHAPTER 9
Transferring Assets to Your Living Trust 115

CHAPTER 10
Executing and Making Changes to Your Living Trust 127

CHAPTER 11
Administering a Living Trust After the Grantor Dies. 133

CHAPTER 12
Ancillary Estate Planning Documents. 141

An Introduction to Living Trusts and Probate

Probate is a an administrative process by which the assets of a deceased person (sometimes called the 'decedent') are gathered; applied to pay debts, taxes, and expenses of administration; and then distributed to the beneficiaries named in the deceased's last will and testament. In most cases, the process is relatively straightforward.

During the past number of years, a lot has been published about the horrors of probate and the necessity to avoid it. We have all heard desperate stories about the outrageous fees charged by lawyers for carrying out probate – something which is often described as a simple administrative task. You have also probably read articles in the newspaper about the ongoing sufferings of families while they wait for prolonged periods to have their loved one's assets released from probate. In practice however, these are only isolated cases for the most part.

Generally speaking, one of the most immediate concerns facing dependents when a loved one passes away is their ability to access funds to cover funeral expenses and to discharge ordinary day-to-day living expenses such as mortgages, educational fees, utility bills, grocery bills and so on. Fortunately, given the variety of probate avoidance measures available, it's easy to ensure that not all your assets are tied up in probate following your death and that your loved ones will have immediate access to funds when they need them most. The most common of these include life insurance policies, pay-on-death accounts, joint tenancies, and trusts.

There is little doubt, however that one of the most popular probate avoidance methods remains the living trust. Indeed, a growing number of elderly people are now turning to living trusts to avoid probate – but not only for this reason. Unlike other probate avoidance methods, a living trust has the added advantage of providing a means by which the creator can provide for the management of his or her property during periods of incapacity as well as ensure the privacy of his or her affairs.

While there are many compelling reasons to avoid probate, including the avoidance of excessive costs and delays, there are also compelling reasons for you to engage in the process. For example, your estate would be afforded protection from creditors after probate is filed. You would also be able to use your will to nominate guardians to care for your minor children after your death. These guardians would normally be affirmed and appointed as part of the probate process. As such, you will need to consider what suits your circumstances. If you ultimately decide that probate avoidance is for you, then there are several probate avoidance measures available to you.

Alternatively, you may choose to have some of your assets go through probate and to have others transfer outside of the probate process. You may even want to allow your entire estate to go through the probate process. The choice is yours.

We will explore several of the most common probate avoidance measures in detail later in this book. However, before we do so, let us start by taking a brief look at what exactly probate is and why people are so keen to avoid it.

CHAPTER 1

Probate – And Why People Try to Avoid It

Overview of Probate & Estate Administration

As mentioned in the Introduction, probate is an administrative process by which the assets of a deceased person are collected, used to discharge debts and taxes and are then distributed to the beneficiaries named in the deceased's last will and testament. If a person dies without making a valid last will and testament, he is said to have died 'intestate' and the related process of distributing his estate is referred to as 'intestate administration' rather than probate. While both processes are relatively similar, with intestate administration, the deceased's possessions are distributed to his heirs in accordance with the succession laws of the state in which he ordinarily resided.

As the administration process is quite like the probate process, people tend to use the word probate interchangeably to describe both processes – despite there being some clear differences between the two.

Steps Involved in Probate

While the steps involved in probating an estate vary from state to state, the process generally involves several key steps. In the first of these steps, the person named as executor in the deceased's will (or a family member or beneficiary) will make an application to the probate court to have the deceased's will admitted to probate and to be formally appointed as executor of his estate. This application usually involves the completion and submission of forms, together with the deceased's will, to the probate court in the county in which the deceased was resident at the time of his death.

Once the application is received, the court will review the will to ensure that it has been validly executed in accordance with state law. If the will is deemed valid, the court will admit it to probate. At the same time, and absent any objections from other interested parties, the court will also formally appoint the person named in the deceased's will as executor of his estate. This appointment is made by issuing a court document to the executor known as "Letters of Authority" or "Letters Testamentary". This document confers on the executor full authority to deal with the deceased's estate.

If the deceased did not make a valid will, a family member will need to petition the court to be appointed as administrator of his estate. The family members entitled to make this application will be determined by state law, which sets out the order in which relatives and creditors of a deceased person are entitled to be appointed as administrator of his estate. The formal appointment of an administrator will be evidenced by the issue of "Letters of Administration" to the administrator.

The next steps in probating or administering a deceased person's estate can be broadly divided into the three steps set out below. For ease of reference, as probate and intestate administration are quite similar, we refer only to probating an estate below.

Step 1 - Collecting and Appraising Assets

One of the first tasks facing an executor following his appointment will be to determine what assets and liabilities the deceased had at the time of his death. To do this, he will need to review the paperwork, bank accounts, legal documents, and financial statements of the deceased, as well as liaise with the deceased's family and business associates. He will also need to contact insurance companies, utility companies, and similar companies to identify the deceased's assets and liabilities. As the executor locates the deceased's assets, he will need to take steps to ensure that control and possession of those assets are transferred to him and that those assets are properly secured and protected against loss or damage.

When it comes to collecting money, financial institutions will normally transfer the proceeds of the deceased's accounts to the executor upon production by the executor of a certified copy of the deceased's death certificate and the executor's letters of authority. The same applies in respect of insurance proceeds due to the deceased's estate following his death. By having control over these funds and control over the deceased's other assets, the executor will be able to discharge the debts and taxes owed by the estate and make the required distributions to the beneficiaries named in the deceased's will.

Step 2 - Paying Taxes and Discharging Debts

Once the executor has collected in and taken control of the deceased's assets, the next step in the process will be to determine what taxes and debts, if any, are owed by the deceased's estate. Having already reviewed the deceased's papers and identified the assets held by the deceased, the executor should have a good understanding of the estate's liabilities.

In the case of debts, the executor will need to write to all the known creditors of the deceased and ask them to provide details and evidence of the debts owed to them. He will also need to place advertisements in local newspapers calling for other creditors of the deceased to come forward within a particular time frame with details of any sums owing to them. If a creditor does not come forward within the required time frame, he will lose the right to claim his debt against the deceased's estate. As the executor receives details of claims against the deceased's estate, he will need to carefully review the merits of each such claim and either accept or reject it. If necessary, the executor can engage the services of an attorney to help determine the validity of claims.

An executor will also need to assess whether any taxes are due by the deceased's estate. Details of the taxes which are likely to be payable are set out in Chapter 8. However, it is often advisable for an executor to have a tax advisor or accountant assist in determining whether taxes are due by the estate.

Once the executor has determined the amount of debts and taxes due by the estate, he will need to ensure that they are properly paid (to the extent there are sufficient assets within the estate to meet such payments). In this regard, the payments will need to be made in a specific order of priority. While this order varies from state to state, it is generally in the following order:

(i)   Costs/expenses of probate administration.

(ii)   Funeral expenses.

(iii) Debts and taxes.

(iv) All other claims.

It is important to emphasize that the executor will not be held personally liable for any debts or taxes which the estate cannot meet, unless of course there has been some wrongdoing on the executor's part – such as fraud.

Step 3 – Transferring Assets

Once all the valid debts and taxes have been paid by the estate, the executor is free to distribute the balance of the estate to the beneficiaries named in the deceased's will. If there is no will, the deceased's estate will be distributed to the deceased's heirs in accordance with state intestacy laws. If there are no living heirs, the estate will 'escheat' and pass to the state treasury.

The executor will generally distribute the deceased's remaining assets in accordance with the terms of his will. However, quite often the executor will have discretion to sell some of the assets of the estate and to distribute cash (quite often this is what is done) rather than specific items of property to the beneficiaries.

In most states, an executor must wait at least six months before distributing any assets to the beneficiaries of the deceased's estate. This waiting period is generally to allow creditors of the deceased's estate to register claims against the estate. Once this waiting period has expired and all bills and taxes paid, the executor is free to distribute the deceased's estate to the relevant beneficiaries/heirs.

After all the assets have been distributed, the executor will need to prepare a final 'settlement' or 'accounting' setting out details of all his dealings in relation to the deceased's estate. The accounting will be presented to the probate court together with evidence of the distributions made by the executor. The court will review the accounting and, subject to it being satisfied that the estate has been administered correctly, it will approve any final distributions to be made by the estate, release the executor from any further duties as executor and close the deceased's estate.

How Long Does Probate Take?

The time it takes to probate an estate will ultimately depend on the assets and liabilities of the deceased and whether his affairs were in order at the time of his death. If the deceased's estate is complicated in some way, such as where there are complicated business structures or tax liabilities, it may take a considerable period of time to determine precisely what assets were held and what debts were owed by the deceased. In such circumstances, it would take longer to discharge any debts and taxes and close the estate. In addition, there may also be difficulties locating beneficiaries named in the deceased's will or challenges made to the legality of the deceased's will or the provisions in it. The occurrence of any of these events will most likely cause a delay in probating the deceased's estate and lead to an increase in the costs of probate.

Each state has its own set of procedures for probate and these will need to be closely followed to probate the deceased's estate. However, in virtually all states, there are different types of probate procedures available for large and small estates. Small estates can usually benefit from streamlined probate procedures and limited court supervision during the probate process. Large estates, on the other hand, take longer to probate and are often subject to close supervision by the courts. Depending on the size of the estate and the probate procedure used, and taking account of other relevant factors, the average probate can take anywhere from 6 months to a year to complete. By way of a simple example, the average time taken to probate an estate in California is 7 to 9 months, if all goes well. Of course, if there are legal challenges to the will, other lawsuits or other problems, this time can be substantially increased. There are in fact probates which have been ongoing for decades!

However, probate should normally be completed within one year from the date on which the application for probate was filed. This period is known as the 'executor's year'. If, for some reason, probate has not been completed within that time frame, the executor may be required to file a status report with the probate court setting out details of what still needs to be done to complete the probate and how much time it's likely to take to do so. If the executor fails to report, the beneficiaries named in the deceased's will can ask the court to make an order requiring the filing of such a report. In addition, they can also ask the court to take any other action it deems necessary to close the probate - including the removal of the existing executor and the appointment of someone else in his place.

How Much Will Probate Cost?

The cost of probate differs from place to place and is generally determined by either state law or custom and practice in a particular area. When all the costs associated with probate are added up, it can easily cost between 1% and 7% (or even more) of the value of the estate in question. As some of these probate costs are set by state law there is often little that you can do to mitigate or reduce them (other than avoid probate of course).

Certain states, such as California, for example, set maximum fees which a lawyer can charge for probating an estate. These maximum fees are based on the gross value of the estate. By gross value, we mean the total value of the estate before any debts or liabilities are subtracted from the estate. As such, these fees can be quite high. For example, consider a case where the principal asset of an estate is a property worth $1 million which has a mortgage of $900,000 secured against it. Even though the net realizable value of the asset is only $100,000, the attorney will be able to charge fees based on the full $1 million value. Based on the fees table below and assuming that there are no other assets in the deceased's estate, the legal fees for probating this asset will be $23,000 notwithstanding that the net value of the asset is $100,000. This represents an effective legal fee of 23% based on the net asset value of the asset.

The table below, which is based on the California probate code, will give you a good idea of likely statutory probate costs. These represent the maximum amounts which a lawyer can charge for probating an estate (assuming that there are no unusual taxes or legal issues associated with the probate).

Estate Value	Statutory Fee
$100,000	$4,000
$200,000	$7,000
$300,000	$9,000
$400,000	$11,000
$500,000	$13,000
$600,000	$15,000
$700,000	$17,000
$800,000	$19,000
$900,000	$21,000
$1,000,000	$23,000
$2,000,000	$33,000

By way of a further illustration, in New York, probate fees of 5% are payable on the first $100,000 in value of the estate, 4% on the next $200,000, 3% on the next $700,000, 2.5% on the next $4 million and 2% on the rest.

In addition to fixed costs such as these, you will also need to be mindful of unanticipated costs. For example, if someone contests the deceased's will or if there is other litigation in relation to the deceased's estate or assets, the costs of probate could rise substantially. Any such costs would be based on the lawyer's hourly charge out rates or a fixed fee agreed with the lawyer.

It is advisable to check the amount of probate fees chargeable in your state. This will help you decide whether there is merit in seeking to avoid having your assets go through probate.

Disadvantages of Probate

We have already touched on two of the biggest drawbacks of the probate process – timing and cost – but there are others.

Once a will is presented to the court it will be filed with the probate office and will be available for inspection by the public at a small cost. As a result, third parties may be able to determine the size of the deceased's estate at the time of his death as well as to whom he passed his assets to. The public availability of this information can have drawbacks in that it is not uncommon for third party service providers to contact beneficiaries offering legal, tax and financial services. Apart from the lack of sensitivity of doing this, the beneficiaries can find it quite intrusive. In addition to this, from a safety and security perspective, it's not helpful to allow random people access details of the names and addresses of people who have received financial windfalls – needless to say, these beneficiaries could become the targets of unscrupulous people.

Advantages of Probate

Despite its many drawbacks, there are some advantages to the probate process. The first of which is guardianship. In his will, a person can nominate a guardian to take care of his minor children following his death. In most cases, the probate court will honor that nomination and officially appoint the nominee as guardian of the deceased's children. Only in rare cases will the court reject a nomination made in a will. If it does, it is usually because the court views the nominated guardian as unsuitable.

Another advantage of the probate process is that, as mentioned, the court imposes a specific period within which creditors must file their claims against the deceased's estate. If a creditor fails to file his claim within the required time frame, his claim becomes 'statute barred' and incapable of being enforced against the deceased's estate. If the deceased died owing only a small amount of debt, this may not be of much assistance. However, if the deceased was, for example, a sole proprietor and had a significant number of business debts owing at the time of his death, it will often make sense to undergo probate if only to reduce the ability of creditors to recover against the estate.

The deceased can also appoint an executor of his choosing to wind up his estate rather than having a court appointed administrator carry out the task. This may be important if the deceased has sensitive information amongst his personal belongings that he does not wish disclosed to his family and friends. A close friend or family member acting as executor may be best placed to ensure the continued privacy of the information in question.

Finally, even where the deceased's estate is structured such that all his assets will avoid probate (we will discuss this further below), it makes sense to have a will. This is to ensure that any assets which are not covered by the probate avoidance techniques, whether intentionally or accidentally, will pass to a person or persons of the testator's choosing. If the estate plan includes a living trust, this will often take the form of a 'pour-over will'. A pour-over will simply transfers all the deceased's assets which end up going through probate to his living trust. It covers situations where the deceased forgot to transfer some of his assets to his living trust or where he received assets shortly before he died and failed to have them transferred to his living trust before he died. Of course, these assets will go through probate but that is often preferable to intestate administration.

Conclusion

While there are many compelling reasons to avoid probate, least of all the excess costs and long delays usually associated with the process, there are also compelling reasons to engage in the process such as the protection given from creditors, the selection of guardians, and the appointment of executors. As such, you will need to consider your individual circumstances and decide what the best approach is for you. If you ultimately decide that probate avoidance is for you, there are several probate avoidance measures available to you. We will discuss these in detail n the next chapter.

Resource

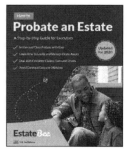

"How to Probate an Estate" is an essential guide for anyone wishing to act as an executor of someone's estate. It takes them step-by-step through the probate process, from the moment the deceased dies to the distribution of the deceased's assets and the closing of the estate, providing the knowledge and confidence to act.

Get your copy at

www.estate-bee.com/product/how-to-probate-an-estate/

CHAPTER 2

Probate Avoidance Measures

Introduction

As you will have gathered from the previous chapter, not all your assets need to go through probate when you die. There are several legal mechanisms that you can use to ensure that some or all those assets pass to your loved ones outside of probate. These include: -

(i)   Setting up pay-on-death, transfer-on-death, or joint accounts.

(ii) Designating beneficiaries under life insurance policies.

(iii) Registering property in joint names with a right of survivorship.

(iv) Creating a revocable living trust.

(v)   Making lifetime gifts.

(vi) Ensuring that the value of your probate estate is such that it allows your executor to avail of a simplified probate procedure for small estates.

If you do not utilize any of the above strategies, or indeed any of the other probate avoidance mechanisms available, your estate may need to go through probate.

Advantages and Disadvantages of Probate Avoidance Measures

We spoke briefly of the advantages and disadvantages of probate in the last chapter. You will need to bear these in mind when deciding whether to allow your estate to go through probate. In the same way, you will also need to look at the individual advantages and disadvantages of each probate avoidance mechanism to ensure it is suitable for your needs.

Probate avoidance measures have several advantages. For example, they are flexible and easy to set up. In many cases, it's simply a case of providing your bank or insurance company with details of the person(s) that you would like to be designated to receive the proceeds of a particular bank account or insurance policy when you die. The financial institution will record those details and the rest will happen automatically. Better still, those designations can be amended or terminated with little difficulty or cost. In fact, a quick trip to your local bank or insurance broker, or to their website, is often all that is required to make these changes. When you die, your designated beneficiaries will usually be able to claim the proceeds of the bank account or insurance policy by presenting a copy of your death certificate to the financial institution in question. That should be sufficient to enable the financial institution to arrange to have the relevant proceeds transferred into the names of your designated beneficiaries.

Of course, there are also disadvantages. In particular, you need to be careful to ensure that all of your probate alternatives are working together to avoid probate (whether in whole or in part) and to distribute your assets in accordance with the overall objectives of your estate plan. In this regard, you need to pay close attention to the beneficiaries named in joint bank accounts and insurance policies; the manner in which real estate is held; the terms of your will and living trust, and the means by which assets are transferred to your living trust. Any lack of attention could result in an asset going to the wrong person and that person receiving a lot more than you had intended to the detriment of someone else. And don't forget, by the time the problem materializes you may not be around to remedy it.

Another disadvantage arises in the case of cost. Sometimes, the cost of establishing and maintaining a living trust, for example, can in fact outweigh the benefits particularly where there is a lot of real estate to transfer to the living trust. As such, it is important that you evaluate the overall costs of using a particular probate avoidance measure before you use it.

To help you evaluate each of the main probate avoidance measures, we take a brief look at them in the ensuing pages. In each case, there will be specific advantages and disadvantages and you will need to pay specific attention to these.

Pay-on-Death Accounts

One of easiest ways for you to transfer assets to someone on your death without getting them tied up in probate is to use a pay-on-death ("POD") account. POD accounts are offered by a variety of financial institutions including banks, savings and loan associations, and credit unions. It is like a normal bank account except that you will add a designation to it identifying the person who will become entitled to the proceeds of that account when you die. A designated beneficiary will simply need to present a certified copy of your death certificate to the bank in question, and it will arrange to have the proceeds transferred to that beneficiary. From a probate perspective, the good news is that these proceeds will pass to the designated beneficiary without the need to go through probate. This allows for a speedy transfer of the funds following your death.

To create a POD account, you can either set up a new POD account with your bank or simply add a POD designation to an existing account. In each case, you will need to provide your bank with details of the proposed beneficiary and sign some standard documents to formally record the designation. Your bank will be able to provide you detailed information on what exactly you need to do all this.

During your lifetime, the designated beneficiary will have no rights whatsoever to access the proceeds of the POD account. In fact, you remain free to (at any time) withdraw the monies in the account, remove the POD designation, change the POD designation, or even close the account. This flexibility is one of the main advantages of using POD accounts in your overall estate plan.

If the designated beneficiary predeceases you, the gift to the beneficiary will usually fail and will not normally be saved by an anti-lapse statute. In which case, the proceeds of the account will become part of your estate for probate purposes. In some cases, it may be possible to designate alternate beneficiaries for your POD account. You should consider doing so and should speak to your bank about this.

Transfer-on-Death Accounts

Transfer-on-death ("TOD") accounts are like POD accounts but are more commonly used to transfer ownership of stocks, securities, bonds, and units in mutual funds.

The Transfer-on-Death Security Registration Act provides for the transfer-on-death of stocks, shares, bonds and other financial instruments and securities. Like the POD accounts, these securities can be transferred on death to named beneficiaries free from the requirement to pass through probate. For more information on designating beneficiaries for your securities, speak to your broker.

To date, the following states have adopted the legislation (with modification in some instances): Alabama, Alaska, Arizona, Arkansas, California, Colorado, Connecticut, Delaware, District of Columbia, Florida, Georgia, Hawaii, Idaho, Illinois, Indiana, Iowa, Kansas, Kentucky, Maine, Maryland, Massachusetts, Michigan, Minnesota, Mississippi, Missouri, Montana, Nebraska, Nevada, New Hampshire, New Jersey, New Mexico, New York, North Carolina, North Dakota, Ohio, Oklahoma, Oregon, Pennsylvania, Rhode Island, South Carolina, South Dakota, Tennessee, Utah, and Vermont.

Only Louisiana and Texas have not adopted the legislation.

If you wish to add a transfer-on-death designation to any of your securities, it is recommended that you speak to a broker.

Retirement Accounts

Again, like POD accounts, it is possible to designate beneficiaries to receive the proceeds of retirement accounts such as IRAs and 401(k)s. As the policy documents relating to retirement accounts are sometimes complex, you should seek the assistance of your broker or financial advisor in making any required designation.

You should also bear in mind that you need to designate the beneficiary or beneficiaries in the account or policy documents themselves – and not in your will, living trust or elsewhere. If you fail to do so, the account proceeds may well end up going through probate. If this happens, they will most likely pass to the person named in your will as residuary beneficiary. Of course, if you die without a valid will, the proceeds will be distributed in accordance with state intestacy laws.

Joint Accounts

Another easy way for you to avoid probate is to have a joint account. A joint account is an account that is held in the name of two or more people and is designated with the right of survivorship. As the account is designated with this right of survivorship, when one of the account holders die, the surviving account holder(s) will automatically acquire the deceased account holder's interest in the account. Whoever is the last surviving joint owner will ultimately own the account outright. Where a transfer on an interest occurs on survivorship, there is no need for probate.

The surviving account holder will simply need to provide a copy of the deceased account holder's death certificate to the bank and the bank can then remove that person's name from the account.

Joint accounts can be used if you want to ensure that your spouse and/or family will have quick and easy access to funds following your death.

Custodial Accounts

People often decide to set aside funds in the form of bank accounts, certificates of deposit or similar securities as a nest egg for their minor children, grandchildren, or others. These funds are often set aside to cover things like college expenses or simply to give children a start in life. One of the most common ways of doing this is by means of a custodial account.

A custodial account is like a trust in many ways but is not technically a trust. With a custodial account, the account holder designates a beneficiary who will be entitled to receive the proceeds of that account when he reaches a specific age. Depending on the state in which the account is established, that age will be determined by either the Uniform Gifts to Minors Act 1956 ("**UGMA**") or the Uniform Transfers to Minors Act 1986 ("**UTMA**"). Until that time arrives, the proceeds or assets (where the account is an investment account) in the account are placed under the management and control of a person known as a custodian. The custodian will have no beneficial interest in the account and will simply manage the account on behalf of the designated beneficiary until he reaches the relevant age. At which point, the custodianship will terminate, and the beneficiary will become entitled to the proceeds or assets within the account. For details of the age upon which custodianships end in your state, see Chapter 7.

Once a custodial account is set up and funded, and the beneficiary named, the proceeds of that account will be deemed to belong to the beneficiary. You will not be entitled to have those proceeds retuned to you nor will you be entitled to any interest generated by the assets in the account – save in some isolated cases. From a probate perspective, this is important as the change of legal and beneficial ownership of the proceeds of the account means that they will not form part of your estate for probate purposes. You will be deemed to have made the gift to the designated beneficiary during your lifetime. When you die, the custodianship will continue as normal until it ultimately terminates when the beneficiary reaches the age set out under the UTMA or UGMA.

Savings Bonds

Saving bonds, like bank accounts, can be held jointly. Also, like POD accounts, they can also contain a pay-on-death designation. In the case of jointly held savings bonds, these will pass to the surviving joint owners on the death of the other bond holders. Similarly, where a POD designation is added to the savings bonds, the bonds will pass to the named beneficiary on the death of the bond holder. In each case, probate will not be needed.

For further information on registering saving bonds in joint names or adding a POD designation, we recommend that you speak to your bank or financial advisor.

Life Insurance Proceeds

A life policy provides yet another example of a simple means by which you can provide for the transfer of assets free from the need for probate. Where you designate a named beneficiary under your life insurance policy, the proceeds of the policy payable on your death will be paid directly to the named beneficiary without the need to go through probate. Of course, if your estate is named as the main beneficiary (which is unusual) or if no beneficiaries have been named or if the named beneficiaries have died before you, the proceeds will be payable to your estate. As such, they will need to pass through probate along with the rest of your probate estate. In which case, the proceeds will pass to the residuary beneficiary unless a specific beneficiary is named in your will to receive the insurance proceeds.

While insurance proceeds payable to a designated beneficiary are not considered part of your estate for probate purposes, they are considered part of your estate for federal estate tax purposes. As such, they may be taxable. This charge to tax (if any) can be avoided by transferring ownership of the policy to another person while you are still alive. If you intend doing this, we recommend that you first speak to a qualified tax advisor.

Joint Ownership of Property

Whether or not real estate owned by you at the time of your death will need to go through probate will depend on how the title to that property was held at the time of your death. Typically, jointly held property can be held in one of four different ways: -

* joint tenancy with a right of survivorship.

- tenancy by the entireties.
- tenancy in common.
- community property.

Each type of property holding is discussed in detail below.

Joint Tenancy with a Right of Survivorship

We have already touched on the concept of joint tenancy in relation to bank accounts. The same principle applies in relation to real estate. Where a property is held under a joint tenancy, each of the property owners has an undivided percentage interest in the entire property. To illustrate this, an example is often useful. So, let us, for example, take a case where four people own a property equally under a joint tenancy arrangement. Each of the four owners has an entitlement to a 25% interest in the entire or whole of the property. However, because each owner has a right to a percentage of the whole, rather than having a divided and defined 25% interest in the property, he is entitled to access and take actions in respect of the entire property and not simply 25% of it.

Where a joint tenant dies, his share passes to the remaining joint tenants. Taking our example again, where one of the four property owners die, his share passes to each of the other three survivors automatically and each of the survivors then becomes entitled to a 33.33% interest in the property. This is an example of the principle of survivorship in operation.

The key point to take from the example above is that the deceased joint owners' share passes to the remaining joint owners without the need for probate. It follows that probate can either be reduced or even eliminated if you convert solely owned assets into jointly owned assets – held under a joint tenancy. This type of ownership permits the jointly owned assets to simply pass directly to the surviving joint owners on the death of one of the owners – without the need for probate.

Tenancy by the Entireties

A special type of joint tenancy known as a 'tenancy by the entirety' is recognized between married couples in certain states. Under this form of joint ownership, if a married couple owns property as tenants in the entirety, then each spouse must obtain the consent of the other before dealing with the property in any way that would affect the rights of the other. This even includes putting in place a mortgage over the property. Each spouse lacks the power to freely dispose of their interest under their will, or in any other way, as the principle of survivorship applies between the spouses.

As the principle of survivorship applies, on the death of the first spouse, the property will pass directly to the surviving spouse without the need for it to go through probate. All that usually needs to be done to register the transfer of property to the sole name of the surviving spouse is to present a certified copy of the deceased spouse's death certificate to the land registry. Once presented, it should update its register to show the surviving spouse as the sole owner of the property.

Important Note

States that recognize a 'tenancy by the entirety' include: Alaska*, Arkansas, Delaware, District of Columbia, Florida, Hawaii, Illinois*, Indiana*, Kentucky*, Maryland, Massachusetts, Michigan*, Mississippi, Missouri, New Jersey, New York*, North Carolina*, Ohio, Oklahoma, Oregon, Pennsylvania, Rhode Island, Tennessee, Utah, Vermont, Virginia and Wyoming.

*States that allow tenancy by entirety for real estate only

Tenancy in Common

A tenancy in common is one of the most common forms of property ownership in most states. A tenancy in common is created where two or more people purchase a property together as 'tenants in common'. As tenants in common, each of the parties own a separate and distinguishable part of the property. To take the example of our four property owners above, if the arrangement was a tenancy in common, each of them would own 25% of the property in their own right and would be free to sell that 25% to any person at any time and/or to dispose of their interest under their will. The right of survivorship does not apply here.

If you hold a share in a property as a tenant in common, it will form part of your estate for probate purposes and you will be free to gift it as you wish under the terms of your will. If you want to ensure that your interest in such a property does not end up going through probate, you could transfer that interest to a revocable living trust (which we will discuss in more detail later) or to a custodial account.

Community Property

Community property states have different rules governing probate, so it is important to understand these rules when planning the distribution of your estate on death.

At the date of writing there are nine community property states in the U.S. namely Arizona, California, Idaho, Louisiana, Nevada, New Mexico, Texas, Washington, and Wisconsin. In Alaska, couples can opt to have their property treated as community property under the terms of a written property agreement. Each of these states has special laws that dictate how married people can own and dispose of property – both real and personal.

Did You Know

Real property is property such as land, buildings, and real estate. Personal property can be broadly defined as including all other property which a person can own – such as cars, boats, cash, jewelry, and art.

In a community property state, the law broadly provides that all earnings generated during a marriage and all property purchased during the marriage is considered community property and therefore equally owned by each spouse. Therefore if, for example, one spouse earns $100,000 per year as an executive, while the other earns $40,000 as a freelance writer, then each spouse shall be deemed to "own" $70,000 of those earnings. In addition to salary, property purchased by one spouse in his or her own name with money he or she earned during the marriage will also be regarded as community property. Similarly, debts incurred by either spouse during their marriage are regarded as debts of the couple rather than those of the individual who incurred it.

Separate property, on the other hand, includes property received by a spouse during their marriage by means of a gift or bequest under a will. It also includes any property owned by a spouse before they got married which that spouse has kept segregated from community property during the marriage. Similarly, all debts incurred by spouses prior to marriage are considered separate debts of each spouse.

Separate property can also include anything that one spouse gives up in favor of the other spouse in writing.

The distinction between community property and separate property becomes important when determining which of a spouse's assets can be freely disposed of by a spouse. In community property states, on the death of a spouse, half of the community property owned by the couple will go to the surviving spouse, unless the deceased spouse's will provides for the transfer of more than half of the community property to the surviving spouse). Otherwise, the deceased spouse is free to dispose of their remaining share of community property as well as their separate property as they see fit.

As the principal of survivorship does not apply to all community property, the property (particularly separate property) would need to be designated with such a right if it is to transfer to a designated beneficiary free from probate. Alternatively, that property can be transferred to a living trust or custodial account. In each case, a beneficiary could be designated to receive the property and probate would not apply.

Revocable Living Trust

An additional way to avoid probate is to establish and fund a revocable living trust.

A revocable living trust is a type of 'inter vivos' (made between the living) trust used for estate planning purposes. Under a revocable living trust arrangement, you create a trust and appoint yourself as trustee of the trust. You then transfer legal ownership of some or all your personal property to the trust. However, as trustee of the trust, you maintain control over and use of the trust property after it has been received by the trust. You can therefore continue to enjoy it in almost the same way as you did when you held the property in your own name.

The trust agreement establishing the trust sets out (in much the same way as a will does) details of the persons who will be entitled to the trust assets following your death. This entitlement may be to specific assets or to a share in the overall trust estate. The agreement also usually entitles you to add assets to or withdraw them from the trust property, change the terms of the trust, change the beneficiaries, make it irrevocable (incapable of change) and even revoke the trust at any time. If the trust is revoked, you will be entitled to the immediate return of the property held by the trust.

After your death, the trust assets will pass to the beneficiaries named in the trust agreement. A person known as the "successor trustee" (which is a little like an executor) will be appointed under the trust agreement and will have the responsibility of transferring ownership of the assets in the trust to the beneficiaries named in the trust agreement. Once all the trust assets have been transferred to the named beneficiaries, the trust ceases to exist.

In most cases, the whole transfer process takes only a few weeks. However, if there is any tax payable, the process may be drawn out. Apart from the benefits associated with a speedy distribution of the trust assets, revocable living trusts are also beneficial from a cost perspective. In many cases, unless real estate needs to be transferred, there are rarely any lawyer or court fees to pay in connection with the winding up of the trust estate.

From a probate avoidance perspective, the most important feature to note about a revocable living trust is that since the assets in the trust are legally owned by the trust, they will not form part of your estate at the time of your death. As such, there will be no need for any of the assets held within the trust to go through the probate process.

Revocable living trusts are quite easy to establish and, apart from avoiding probate, there are many other advantages to using living trusts as part of your overall estate plan. These reasons relate to the management of your assets during incapacity, privacy, and in some cases taxes.

We will discuss revocable living trusts in greater detail later in this book.

Lifetime Gifts

It most likely goes without saying but giving away property while you are still alive helps avoid probate since anything that you don't own at the time of your death cannot go through the probate of your estate.

Probate Free Transfers of Assets

In some states, like New Jersey, ownership of vehicles which are solely owned by you at the time of death may be transferred immediately to your surviving spouse/partner or next of kin without the need for probate – provided that the transfer occurs before probate commences. Such vehicles can include trucks, motor homes and boats provided the total value of the vehicle in question does not exceed the amount specified under state law for such transfers. In most cases that amount will vary between $25,000 and $75,000 depending on the laws of the deceased's state of residence.

The state's department of motor vehicles can tell you whether the vehicles can be transferred without the need for probate and what needs to be done to carry out the transfer. Once your spouse or next of kin can legally transfer the vehicle the department will, on presentation of a copy of your death certificate, transfer the title of the vehicle to that person.

In addition to vehicles, any salary, wages, accumulated vacation and sick benefits, plus any other fringe benefits, may according to the laws of certain states be paid to your surviving spouse/partner, adult children or next of kin without the need for probate. The department of labor should be able to tell you whether these procedures apply in your state and, if so, your employer should be able to assist your family with the process generally when the time comes. If you are in any doubt as to your rights or as to those of the proposed beneficiaries of your estate, you should contact an attorney licensed in your state.

If, for whatever reason, the vehicle or wages (as the case may be) are not transferred before probate commences, the assets may be deemed to form part of your estate and will need to go through probate. The problem with allowing this is that your spouse or next of kin may not be the beneficiaries of these items under your will. As such, they may lose out on a valuable opportunity to acquire these assets, reduce the size of your probate estate and reduce the related costs of probate which, as mentioned, tend to be based on the value of the probate estate. Therefore, any such transfers should preferably be made at the earliest opportunity following your death.

Simplified Transfer Procedures for "Small Estates"

The laws in most states allow for the transfer of 'small estates' in a simple, cheap and efficient manner outside of the main probate process. While the definition of a 'small estate' varies from state to state, it can be generally defined as an estate:

(i)   which has a total value below a certain financial amount; and/or

(ii)   in which the bulk of the estate assets will be either transferred by operation of law to the surviving family members of the deceased or used to pay the debts associated with the deceased's last illness.

If your estate is deemed to be a 'small estate' for the purposes of state law, it will normally be possible to transfer the assets within your estate to your beneficiaries or heirs using one of two streamlined transfer procedures. These procedures include a 'small estate affidavit' procedure and a 'summary administration' procedure.

For your estate to qualify as a small estate, its value will need to be below a certain amount. This amount varies from state to state and currently ranges from estates with net values as low as $500 to as high as $500,000, depending on the state. In some states this simplified procedure will not be available if you die owning any real estate, irrespective of the value of that real estate.

If the value of your estate is under the threshold for small estates, a simple affidavit or certification procedure can be used thereby avoiding a lengthy and costly probate administration procedure. However, as most people generally have a home or land valued in excess of their state's "small estate" value, many people are unable to avail of this exemption from the probate process.

Resource

EstateBee's **Estate Planning Essentials** introduces you to some of the devices used in estate planning such as wills, trusts, powers of attorney, medical directives, transfer on death accounts and more. Particular attention is paid throughout to beneficiaries, children, disinheritance, incapacity, and taxes. You will learn everything necessary to enable you to put an effective estate plan in place, without the need or cost of lawyers.

Get your copy at

www.estate-bee.com/product/estate-planning-essentials/

CHAPTER 3

An Introduction to Trusts

What Exactly Is a Trust?

We've all heard of national trusts, land trusts, boards of trustees at schools and colleges, as well as trust estates, trust property, unit trusts (investments), steel trusts (monopolies), trust accounts, trust deeds... it seems that trusts are all around us. What is more, the list of different trust types seems to be diverse — do they all have something in common?

The short answer is "yes". We will look at these common components of a trust in the ensuing pages. At the same time, we will take a brief look at trust law and trusteeship as it's important that you understand the general concept of trusts before we move into a more detailed discussion of revocable living trusts.

A trust can be described as a fiduciary arrangement whereby one or more persons become the legal owner(s) of trust property, which they hold not on their own behalf but for the use and benefit of somebody else.

Important Note

A trust is a legal device established by a person, usually under written agreement, and used to manage real or personal property for the benefit of another.

Every trust has several core components. These include: -

(i)   The *grantor* (also called a settlor, donor, or creator) - the person who creates the trust.

(ii)   The *objective* of the trust – why it has been set up.

(iii) The *trust property* – the property which has been placed into the trust.

(iv) The *trustee* – the person who will manage the trust property.

(v)   The *beneficiaries* – the people entitled to receive the trust property.

(vi) The *rules* of the trust.

These 'core elements' must be contained in every trust. Usually, the terms of the trust are set out in either a trust agreement (sometimes called a trust declaration) or a will, which in the case of a trust agreement is created by the grantor or, in the case of a will, by the testator.

Under the terms of a trust, a grantor 'settles' trust property on one or more trustees for the benefit of one or more beneficiaries. The trustee, in turn, assumes an obligation to preserve and protect the trust property and generally manage the trust's affairs and assets, in accordance with the trust's rules, on behalf of the beneficiaries.

The standard of care that a trustee must observe in carrying out his or her obligation is one of the highest known to the law. A trustee must always act for the benefit of and in the best interests of the beneficiaries of the trust, and never for his or her own personal gain. The trustee must also exercise due care and diligence in the management of the trust property.

The obligation of the trustee extends to vesting or transferring the trust property to the beneficiaries upon the happening of a future event (e.g. when the grantor dies, or when the beneficiaries attain a specific age, complete college or satisfy whatever conditions are set out in the trust document).

Trust property can be any form of property, including cash, real estate, and every type of personal property. The trust agreement (or the will) basically just says what the trustee can do, cannot do, and must do. It may also define who can be a beneficiary and who cannot.

The Origin of Trusts

The ancient Romans formulated a legal principle known as the fidei commissa (meaning that which is "faithfully committed" or "a faithful performance") which is a precursor to the modern-day trust arrangement.

However, trust law, as most western countries know it, developed in England at the time of the Crusades, during the 12th and 13th centuries. Prior to the invention of freehold (where you own the property as well as the land it's built on), land was held under the feudal system, where various "rents" and services (including the raising of troops, provision of horses, weaponry, fodder, etc.) were owed either to the king, or to the noble above you in the feudal hierarchy, as the price for your landholding.

When landed knights went on crusade, they were often away for years, sometimes leaving only a poorly educated bailiff to look after things at home. This, as you can imagine, caused a variety of difficulties. Over time, some of the landed gentry began to convey their holdings to a more skilled custodian during their absence. This person would perform their feudal obligations, and generally keep the farm and estate running. It was mutually agreed that the custodian would sell the land back to the knight upon his return. However, not all custodians did the right thing, leaving the knight to petition the king for justice. The Lord Chancellor was delegated to handle these cases, and he eventually set up the Court of Chancery to hear them. This court was empowered to reach decisions based not just on the strict letter of the law, but on principles of fairness and equity which themselves in time became law.

From these and similar small beginnings, the legislators in Parliament, plus the King's Executive Council and the equity court itself (the Court of Chancery) developed a whole new branch of law, a major part of which was the law of "uses" — as trusts were originally called.

Living trusts, which date back to the 16th century, developed from this law of uses when landowners used trusts to circumvent the King's intervention in succession (inheritance) matters. Kings often concerned themselves with overseeing the distribution of property when large landowners died — in fact, that process of overseeing transfers was really the first form of probate.

So, what could the landowners do to get around this? By deeding their properties to the Church (in exchange for the promise that the Church would "grant" the land back to the landowner's heirs when they died) the landowner was able to avoid the probate process of the King altogether.

Probate and trusts made the long trip to America amongst the papers of some of the first British settlers, who brought English customs and laws with them. Today, trusts are legal in all states in America, and in many other countries.

Basic Types of Trusts

For estate planning, there are two principal types of trust that you need to be aware of. These are testamentary trusts and living trusts. A testamentary trust is simply a trust created under the terms of a person's will and only comes into effect when that person dies. A living trust, on the other hand, is created and comes into effect during the grantor's lifetime.

Since living trusts are created under the terms of a declaration (a written agreement between two or more parties) during the grantor's lifetime, they can be stated to be revocable or irrevocable during the grantor's lifetime. A revocable trust is a trust that can be amended or terminated by the grantor at will. With revocable living trusts, the grantor reserves the right to amend the terms of the trust, to call for the return of the assets in the trust and even to terminate the trust – at will. This right exists right up until the time the grantor dies. At that point, the trust becomes irrevocable and cannot be varied or amended. Similarly, where the grantor creates an irrevocable living trust at the outset, the grantor will not be able to amend its terms or even terminate the trust at any point. Unless there is some specific reason (such as obtaining a tax relief or providing for a settlement on divorce, for example) for creating an irrevocable living trust, it is normally recommended that they are avoided due to their inflexibility.

What Exactly Are Living Trusts?

When we talk about "living trusts", we're simply emphasizing the fact that the people involved in creating the trust — the grantor and trustee — are both alive at the time the trust is created – unlike a trust created under a will (known as a testamentary trust) which only comes into existence when the testator (the person making the will) dies. For this reason, lawyers sometimes use the old Latin term "inter vivos", meaning 'between or among the living', when talking about living trusts.

Did You Know ?

Living trusts are also known as 'inter vivos trusts' or 'family trusts.'

A living trust is an arrangement which is created for the simple purpose of holding ownership of a person's assets outside of his estate during his lifetime, and distributing those assets after his death in accordance with the terms of his living trust agreement. It is created by simply executing a living trust agreement or trust instrument. Under the agreement, the grantor will appoint himself as trustee of that trust and will set out who the beneficiaries of the trust assets (sometimes called a 'trust estate') are and the specific portion of those assets that each such beneficiary will become entitled to on his death.

Once the living trust agreement has been signed and the living trust thereby created, the grantor will transfer property from his personal ownership to the trust. While the legal ownership of the trust property changes, the grantor (as trustee) still maintains control over the property and can continue to enjoy it in same way as he did prior to transferring it to the trust. This is one of the unique and most attractive features of a revocable living trust.

As living trusts are ordinarily revocable, the grantor reserves the right to revoke or terminate the trust and resume personal ownership of the trust property at any time. In addition, he also maintains the right, exercisable at his discretion, to add to or withdraw assets from the trust property, to change the terms of the trust and even to make it irrevocable at some time in the future.

After the grantor (or the grantor and his/her spouse in the case of a joint living trust) dies, the trust agreement identifies the person who will act as successor trustee. A successor trustee is the person appointed by the grantor under the terms of the trust agreement to manage the distribution of the trust property to the beneficiaries upon the death of the grantor. In many respects, a successor trustee plays a similar role to that of an executor appointed under a will.

In some cases, such as where the beneficiary is the surviving spouse of the grantor, the whole transfer process may take much less time than probating a will and this efficiency should help minimize any attorney fees associated with the transfer of the trust assets and the winding up of the trust. The living trust ceases to exist when all the trust property has been transferred to the beneficiaries.

Parties to a Living Trust

While the parties to a living trust are pretty much the same as those which are party to a normal trust, it's worth having a quick look at them at this juncture so that you can familiarize yourself with them.

The principal parties are as follows: -

Grantor/Settlor   This is the person who sets up the trust.

Trustee   This is the person who will manage the trust property. When it comes to revocable living trusts, the grantor usually acts as trustee.

Successor Trustee   The successor trustee is the person who will step-in to manage the trust property when the grantor dies or if the grantor becomes incapacitated. When the grantor dies, the successor trustee will distribute the assets in the trust in accordance with the terms of the living trust agreement. He or she will not have any power to amend or vary the terms of the trust agreement in any way.

Beneficiaries   These are the people who are entitled to receive the benefit of the benefit of the trust's assets. During the grantor's lifetime, this will also usually include the grantor. When he dies, other beneficiaries will be entitled to receive the assets. In the case of a revocable living trust, the grantor is free to change the beneficiaries at any time.

The Development and Growing Use of Living Trusts

Revocable living trusts have grown rapidly in popularity in the recent years. They are being increasingly seen as a wiser alternative to the traditional will. When prepared properly living trusts can avoid probate, avoid or reduce legal fees, save on taxes, preserve your privacy and prevent a court having a say in the control of some of your assets if you become incapacitated. We discuss incapacity in more detail in later chapters.

For all these reasons, the use of revocable living trusts has grown rapidly over the past several decades, and it is likely that the popularity of living trusts will continue for years to come.

CHAPTER 4

Advantages and Disadvantages of Living Trusts

Advantages of Using a Living Trust

There are many different and distinct advantages associated with the use of living trusts. However, whether any of these advantages would benefit you really depends on your circumstances. To assist you with making that determination, we have set out below a summary of each of the primary advantages that a living trust could offer you. Each section describes an advantage in detail and will help you decide if that living trust advantage would benefit you.

Avoids Probate

As already discussed, if you leave assets to beneficiaries under the terms of your will, those assets will normally need to go through the probate process before they can be transferred to your beneficiaries. Unfortunately, there are costs and delays associated with probate. The level of these costs and delays vary from case to case depending on the circumstances surrounding the probate in question.

In many cases, probate will result in your beneficiaries not being able to receive their inheritances until the probate process has completed – of course there are some exceptions in that not all assets need to go through the probate process (see Chapter 2). However, any delay in the probate of your estate – which is likely in many cases - could cause your family and beneficiaries both financial and emotional distress in the intervening period.

Consider for a moment if you were the sole 'bread winner' in the household and, after your passing, your family had to wait a year or more to gain access to your assets (including bank accounts) – how would your family pay the mortgage or pay for your children's education? Believe it or not, these are very real concerns for many American families.

Add to this the fact that if there is a delay in formally appointing an executor under your will, due to a challenge to your will, for example, your family may be powerless to manage some of the assets within your estate. Let us for a moment assume that you are the sole owner of a restaurant or shop at the time of your passing. During the period between your death and the issue of letters of authority to your executor, your nominated executor (as well as your family) will not have the legal authority to manage, sell or even liquate the business. This inability to act in relation to the business during this period could have a detrimental impact on the valuation and future success of the business and, in turn, on the value of the assets to be passed to your heirs.

The above principle applies to investment accounts, shareholdings, property portfolios, etc., in the same way it applies to a business.

Important Note

Avoiding probate can be a major benefit if you own real estate outside your state of residence. This is because owners of out-of-state property often must have that property probated in the state in which the property is located. These proceedings are known as ancillary probate proceeding. With these additional probate proceedings come additional filings, fees, and maybe even a different lawyer to carry out the probate in that state. If, however, that real estate was to be transferred to your living trust, then on your death, the property could be transferred in the same way as a normal conveyance without the need for the ancillary probate.

Fortunately, many of the difficulties identified in the above scenario can be avoided if you place some or all your assets into a living trust. Remember, assets which you place into your living trust will not be part of your probate estate upon your death. As such, those assets can be distributed following your death according to the terms of the living trust agreement without the need for a court to oversee the distributions in a manner similar to that in which it oversees distributions made as part of the probate process. This will result in a much quicker distribution of assets to the beneficiaries and will mean that the successor trustee named in your living trust can take immediate control of the trust assets upon your death.

Saves Money

By avoiding probate, you will also save your heirs a substantial amount of money in filing fees, costs, attorney fees and executor fees. For example, in California both the executor and an attorney can receive the following fixed fees for probate:

* Up to 4% of the first $100,000 of the estate = $4,000
* Up to 3% of the next $100,000 of the estate = $3,000
* Up to 2% of the next $800,000 of the estate = $16,000

In respect of an estate worth $1 million, each could be entitled to a total fee of $23,000. In other words, your heirs could have to pay up to $46,000 in executor and attorney's fees alone. On top of this, they would still need to pay other costs to probate your estate such as filing fees, valuation fees, etc. The estate would also have to pay any debts and taxes due by it.

While we have just looked at California in the example above, many other states have similar types of fees. The monetary benefit of avoiding probate is therefore clear.

Avoids Publicity

Another potential benefit is that your family will not have to put up with any unwanted publicity like that which could arise in relation to probate. Remember, with probate, your will (and possibly a schedule of all your assets) is filed in the probate registry and becomes a public document open for inspection for anyone upon payment of a small fee. By contrast, a living trust is a private contract entered into between you (as grantor) and you (as trustee) and, as there is no public filing requirement, can therefore remain confidential. No one other than those named in your trust agreement need become aware of the existence of the trust, the assets you have, to whom you have passed those assets, who exactly you owed money to and what arrangements you put in place for your family. Of course, the successor trustee will need to show the trust agreement (or extracts of it) to banks and other financial institutions in order to manage the distribution of the trust assets – but it nevertheless remains relatively private with few people having knowledge of what you had and to whom you passed it on your death.

This is an important protection when it comes to creditors of your estate and, sometimes more importantly, creditors of the beneficiaries of your trust. Remember, with probate, the contents of your will can be viewed by virtually anyone including creditors. Moreover, your will often describes the extent, location, and value of the assets in your estate. This information of course makes it a lot easier for creditors to assess and make claims against your estate. Similarly, if a creditor of one of your beneficiaries sees that an asset is going to your beneficiary, that creditor might be more likely to take a claim against your beneficiary.

While there is nothing wrong with the lawful recovery of debts, the information that is made available to the public can reduce your executor's bargaining power when it comes to settling debts with your creditors – why would they accept anything less if they know from public records that you have a large solvent estate? Moreover, given that the estate is solvent, it would also encourage other would-be litigants to consider suing the estate for alleged wrongdoings. The same concern applies equally to your beneficiaries.

On top of all this, it's a well-known practice that service providers such as brokers, financiers and, dare we say, even lawyers often monitor probates and subsequently offer their services to beneficiaries who have received large amounts of assets. These types of offers can be an unwelcomed invasion of privacy to your loved ones at a time when they are emotionally hurt and vulnerable. Again, your beneficiaries' privacy needs to be protected.

As you can see from the above, there is a significant benefit in maintaining your privacy. This protection can be provided by a living trust, but it is not always guaranteed. If, for example, any litigation ensues following your death, the trust document could be produced as evidence in a court hearing and can, in a similar way to a will, become public.

Finally, in certain cases, where title to land or buildings is transferred to a living trust, a financial institution holding security over the property may require that a copy of the living trust be filed together with the transfer deed in the county clerk's office. As a result, the living trust could become a matter of public record. If there is no security over the property, this specific issue should not arise.

As you will have seen, while privacy can be protected to a large degree, there are still some potential risks. As such, you should bear these in mind if privacy is the main reason for you using a living trust.

Provides Protection During Incapacity

A growing number of older Americans are putting their most valuable assets into living trusts because they want to avoid them being placed under the management of a court-appointed guardian or conservator (we'll call both a 'guardian' for convenience) if they become unable to manage their affairs. Unfortunately, in the absence of appointing this guardian, your family will more likely than not be unable to manage your affairs legally or practically.

The appointment of a court-appointed guardian is by no means a simple process. It will normally require your family to go to court and, in a public hearing, declare you incompetent and/or incapacitated, and request that the court appoint a guardian to manage your affairs. This can often be a time-consuming and costly process, as well as an emotionally difficult one for your family.

Resource

Make Your Own Medical & Financial Powers of Attorney

Powers of attorney allow people you trust to manage your property and financial affairs during periods in which you are incapacitated; as well as make medical decisions on your behalf based on the instructions in your power of attorney document. This ensures that your affairs do not go unmanaged if you are incapacitated and you do not receive any unwanted medical treatments.

This book provides all the necessary documents and step-by-step instructions to make a power of attorney to cover virtually any situation. Get your copy at **www.estate-bee.com/product/make-your-own-medical-financial-powers-of-attorney**

Fortunately, there are other options available to you. Both a durable general power of attorney and a living trust can be used to provide for the management of your affairs during periods of incapacity. Under a durable general power of attorney, you can delegate authority to an agent to manage your affairs. This authority will typically extend to allow your agent collect and disburse money on your behalf; operate your bank accounts; buy and sell property in your name; refurbish and rent out your property; and generally sign documents and deeds as your alter ego. It permits your agent to act as your authorized legal representative in relation to the whole cross-section of your legal and financial affairs until such time as the authorization granted under the power of attorney is revoked or comes to an end. This authorization normally comes to end when you regain mental capacity or die.

On the other hand, with a properly drafted living trust, if you become disabled or otherwise unable to manage your estate, your living trust avoids the need for a court-mandated conservatorship by nominating a person known as a successor trustee (similar to a guardian) to manage the trust assets during any period of incapacity. This, however, only applies to assets held in the trust.

If other assets are held outside the terms of the trust, it may still be necessary to apply to court to have a guardian/conservator appointed to manage those assets if you have not made a durable general power of attorney.

Important Note

With increasing security precautions being introduced by financial institutions, the effectiveness of powers of attorney has been gradually eroded over the last number of years. Institutions are increasingly reluctant to allow people access to another's account on the mere presentation of a power of attorney. For the most part, this problem is not as prevalent with living trusts. This is because the account will normally not be in your individual name but rather in the trust's name. The financial institution would (or at least should) have obtained a copy of the trust agreement or trust instrument when setting up the account and should therefore already have details of the trustee (you) and the successor trustee to hand. This tends to make it easier for the successor trustee to gain access to the trust account - upon production of standard documentation (to evidence your death or incapacity) and identification to the financial institution.

Trust law imposes strict obligations and responsibilities on persons acting as trustees – including your successor trustee. In carrying out their duties, trustees are required to exercise a higher standard of prudence and performance than one who is dealing with property in their own right.

Moreover, without the express written permission of the grantor, the trustee cannot use trust property for any purposes other than those specified in the trust document itself. In other words, the scope of authority granted to a trustee to act on behalf of the trust is limited by the 'dos and don'ts' of the trust agreement. By placing restrictions on the trustee in this way, the grantor can exercise a degree of control over what the trustee can and cannot do. This ensures (in so far as it is legally possible) that the trustee will act for the benefit of the beneficiaries. Remember, when a successor trustee is appointed, on the death of the grantor or during a period of incapacity of the grantor, he will be bound by the same trust rules as the trustee.

Difficult to Contest

One of the often-overlooked benefits of a living trust is that its privacy makes it much more difficult to contest by comparison to a will. With a will, beneficiaries and heirs can become upset with their inheritances and often hire attorneys to contest the will. The probate process often commences by convening a court hearing that gives disgruntled heirs a venue to contest the will. Also, the public nature of the will makes it cost efficient and easy for an attorney to review the will and evaluate the likelihood of a successful challenge being made to its validity or its terms before deciding whether or not to take the case. However, with a living trust, the contents are not publicly known. As such, attorneys are less likely to spend their own time and money pursuing a lawsuit with unknown probabilities of success.

It follows that a living trust can be a very useful device especially if you want to disinherit a child or relative; or if you think there may be a disagreement over the distribution of your estate or even a challenge to your will. However, this is not the only protection if affords. It's considered more difficult to challenge a living trust on the grounds of competency than a will as any continuing involvement on your part in managing the trust assets would suggest that you were able to competently manage your affairs and that you intended to manage your affairs in accordance with the terms of the trust — therefore making your competency difficult to contest.

Management of Children's Inheritance

If you are concerned about the future welfare of your children in the event that you die before they reach an age where they can manage inheritances that they receive, you can set up one or more separate child sub-trusts or custodianships within your living trust for the benefit of each child. A child sub-trust is usually set up to fund a child's education, upkeep, and other needs. A custodianship is like a trust in that it provides for the management of gifts made to children until they are old enough to receive them.

Both a custodianship and child sub-trust are easy to establish under a living trust. In each case, you simply make a gift to the child under the living trust. In turn, the terms of the living trust will usually provide that the child will not inherit the property from the trust until he or she reaches a specified age. Until the child or children reach the designated age, the successor trustee or a named custodian will manage the trust property on the child's behalf. The grantor is free to designate any age he wishes when using a child sub-trust, but this age is often between 18 and 30 years. By contrast, the ages which can be set in respect of custodianships are prescribed under state law and, in most cases, specify a particular age at which the custodianship automatically comes to an end.

Living trusts therefore provide an extremely useful mechanism for managing assets passed to minors and young adults. We discuss property management for children in greater detail in Chapter 7.

Flexible

One of the most important advantages of a living trust is that they are extremely flexible. In the normal course, you can change the terms of the trust, change the beneficiaries, or even change the successor trustee as you wish. Moreover, you can add new assets to the trust at any time or even call for the return of some or all the trust assets that you have already put into the trust. You can even terminate the trust at your absolute discretion.

All that is usually needed to make changes to your trust is a simple amendment agreement. Changes regarding the identity of assets held in the trust can sometimes be made by simply updating the schedule to the trust agreement.

Inexpensive and Easy to Create

Living trusts also have the added advantage of being quite easy to set up and operate. To create a basic living trust, you simply sign a document called a 'Declaration of Trust' or a 'Revocable Living Trust Agreement'. You then name yourself as trustee of the trust and transfer whatever assets or property you wish into that trust. We will cover the set-up process in more detail later in this book.

And while you can have a lawyer set up a living trust for you, it certainly is not necessary. You can quite easily do it yourself by using some of the forms attached to this book or some of the other living trust packs currently available online. Just make sure you buy from a reputable vendor (like EstateBee).

Peace of Mind

A living trust can give you peace of mind in several ways. During your lifetime, you will always have the comfort of knowing that you can change the terms of your living trust and even call for the return of your assets at any time. In addition, you would have the comfort of knowing that if an accident or illness left you incapacitated your family would not be left helpless to manage your trust assets. Rather, your nominated successor trustee would be able to step-in and manage your trust estate for you.

You and your family will also have the comfort of knowing that, following your death, proper arrangements have been made for the management of your children's inheritance until they reach a sufficient age to manage it on their own behalf. Also, your family will have very quick access to your assets and should not have to wait for a prolonged period to receive the vital resources that they need. Your family will be spared the difficult task of dealing with attorneys (to a large degree at least) and attending probate court proceedings.

Disadvantages of Living Trusts

While, for many reasons, the advantages associated with the use of living trusts receive most of the public attention, the disadvantages should also be taken into consideration. We explore some of the most common disadvantages below.

Failure to Fund the Living Trust

One of the main problems associated with living trusts is facilitating the transfer of assets into the trust itself. This act of transferring assets is commonly referred to as 'funding the trust'. Despite establishing a trust many people fail to transfer any assets into the trust or incorrectly believe that they have in fact transferred assets into the trust.

There are many different types of asset which can be transferred to your trust including stocks, bonds, mutual funds, bank accounts, real estate, life insurance policies, vehicles, boats, and personal belongings – anything of value really. The problem is that if any of these assets have forms of 'title documents' associated with them, you must ensure that the title is properly transferred from your personal name into the name of the trust using the correct title document.

For example, if you want to transfer real estate to your living trust, you will need to have your lawyer prepare appropriate transfer documentation to legally transfer the title to that real estate to your trust. Instead of "John Smith" being the registered owner of the real estate, "John Smith as trustee of the John Smith Trust" will become the registered owner. The same principle applies to bank accounts, stocks, and all other assets with title documents. Personal belongings such as jewelry, which does not have a title deed, can be transferred by simply including a detailed description of it in the schedule to your trust agreement - more on this later.

Unfortunately, people often have their attorney prepare a living trust or prepare it themselves using an off-the-shelf kit and incorrectly assume that all of their assets will automatically be distributed in accordance with the terms of their trust. Of course, the trust cannot transfer assets that it does not legally have. This can often result in the need for intestate administration proceedings if the grantor has failed to make a will to deal with assets not transferred to the trust. The bottom line is that if you create a trust, not alone must you be prepared to fund it, you must fund it. Otherwise the exercise may end up being a waste of time, money, and effort.

Does not Completely Avoid Delays in Distribution of Assets

One of the principal reasons for delays in the probate process is caused by the necessity to resolve complicated tax issues before distributing assets to the beneficiaries of the deceased person's estate.

An executor of your estate will not be inclined to carry out all your required distributions under your will until he knows the full extent of your tax liability. While this generally takes about six months to determine, it can sometimes take up to eighteen months to resolve if your affairs are complex. More unfortunate, however, is the fact that the same problem arises in relation to a living trust as you will be taxed as if the living trust does not exist (more on this later). As such, in the same way that your executor will refrain from distributing assets before determining your tax position, so too will your successor trustee.

Another common problem stems from the collection of assets, in particular life insurance proceeds. It can sometimes take several months to obtain these proceeds, and again the problem exists both for an executor appointed under a will and a successor trustee appointed under a living trust.

So, while a living trust is not going to eliminate delays caused by tax issues or the collection of certain assets, it can speed up the distribution process in respect of other assets due to the lack of court intervention over the acts of the trustee. This should therefore go some way towards quickening the distribution process. Although, it should be borne in mind that most people's tax affairs are relatively straightforward, and most insurance companies pay out life insurance proceeds relatively quickly.

Lack of Court Supervision

As outlined above, one of the benefits of the probate system is that the court watches over the distribution of your estate and, in doing so, protects the interests of your estate's beneficiaries. However, no such supervision occurs with a living trust as the responsibility for effecting and overseeing the distribution of your trust assets rests solely with your designated successor trustee. This can be disadvantageous in circumstances. For example, if you believe that there is likely to be a significant dispute in relation to your assets or if you do not trust anyone enough to act as your successor trustee, it may be worth considering allowing those assets to go through the probate process or appointing a professional trustee as successor trustee. At least then, you will have the peace of mind of knowing that a probate court judge will oversee the transfer of your assets in accordance with the terms of your will and your wishes; or that a professional trust company will distribute the trust assets in accordance with the trust agreement.

No Real Tax Savings

Despite what many people are led to believe, there is little tax advantage to be gained by placing your assets in a living trust. The real money saver relates to savings on probate fees.

When we talk about tax and living trusts, we are referring to two specific types of tax namely income tax and federal estate tax. We will look at each in turn.

(i)   Income Tax

When you create a revocable living trust, you retain the right to amend the terms of the trust, call for the return of any assets that you have transferred to the trust and even terminate the trust. Because you have this vast level of control, federal tax laws still regard you as the owner of the trust property – just under a different guise. As a result, you must report any income made by the trust on your own annual income statement and, more importantly, pay income tax on those earnings.

If you are acting as the trustee of your own living trust, there is no need to obtain a separate employer identification number – this is like a social security number. However, if you die or become incapacitated and someone else is acting as trustee of your trust (such as your successor trustee), they may need to obtain an identification number from the Internal Revenue Service (IRS) for the trust and thereafter make income tax returns on behalf of the trust.

You will make your own income tax filings using IRS Form 1040 whereas the trust will make its return using IRS Form 1041.

Where the trust is paying taxes using its own tax identification number, which will happen when the successor trustee steps-in to manage the trust assets, it will be obliged to pay income tax on income earned by the trust and not distributed to the beneficiaries. The beneficiaries, in turn, will be obliged to pay income tax on any income they receive from the trust. The income tax rates for trusts are like an individual's tax rate save that the threshold at which a trust pays the higher rate of income tax is lower than that for individuals.

(ii) Estate Tax

Similar to the position with income tax, as you will be deemed to be in control of the trust, your trust will be deemed to be part of your estate and will be subject to estate tax in the normal way. Whether any estate tax will have to be paid will depend on the value of your estate. For more information on estate tax, see Chapter 8.

The bottom line is that if you control your living trust then either you or your estate will pay income and/or estate taxes on the assets held in the trust – just as if they were not in the trust. There is simply no inherent tax advantage to placing assets in a living trust. However, they can be used to enable you to prudently avail of your available tax-free transfer thresholds in the same way as a will can be used. We will discuss this further in Chapter 5.

Limited Financial Savings for Smaller Estates

While living trusts are often stated to be viable alternatives to incurring the costs associated with writing a will and having your assets go through probate, this is not always true. The real determination as to whether a living trust will save you money depends on the value of your estate as this value will determine the probate fees payable by your estate. If your estate has a small monetary value, you may find that the probate fees payable in your state are quite low. Moreover, you may even find that your estate may be able to avail of one of the simplified probate procedures available for small estates.

The cost of writing a will and probating an estate needs to be contrasted to the costs associated with having a living trust. The costs of transferring your assets to and from your trust need to be considered as well as the cost of monitoring your overall estate plan from year to year. In addition, if someone other than you is acting as trustee, you may also have to pay trustee fees.

However, if the additional costs associated with a living trust are within the normal cost parameters for this type of work, then the benefits often outweigh the associated costs. You will need to sit down and work these issues out before you create your trust.

No Protection from Creditors

Despite what many people believe, placing your assets in a revocable living trust does not generally protect them from attack by your creditors. In the same way as trusts are transparent for tax reasons, your creditors have a right to go after those assets as if they were still legally in your name.

There are some exceptions to the general principle above. For example, if you place your assets into an irrevocable living trust (as opposed to a revocable living trust), creditors will find it difficult to attack the trust in respect of debts which arose after the date on which the assets were transferred to the trust. Of course, the problem with using irrevocable living trusts is that the assets placed into the trust are locked in and you cannot easily get them out.

A similar principle could apply when you die. This is because, on your death, your revocable living trust becomes irrevocable. The laws in some states may, depending on the laws governing the trust and the circumstances surrounding the placing of assets in that trust, protect the now irrevocable living trust from attack by creditors. For more information on this, speak to your attorney.

One of the principal drawbacks of not having your estate go through the probate process is that no time limit is imposed on creditors within which they can take claims against your estate. With probate, all creditors must notify the executor of any claim they have against your estate within a specific time frame set out under state law. If they fail to do so, their claim against your estate becomes statute barred and they will be unable to recover the debts due to them. The opposite situation applies in relation to living trusts. As no cut-off time is imposed on your creditors, they will be free to take claims against your estate well after you have died. This is also true of your living trust. In fact, even after your living trust has distributed it assets and has been wound up, your creditors maintain the right, in many states, to sue the beneficiaries of those assets for the debts you owed – up to a maximum amount equal to the benefit they received from the living trust.

For the reasons outlined above, it is often beneficial to open a probate case simply to restrict the rights of your creditors to take action against your estate. You can generally do this even where your estate has little or no assets. By doing this, the protection afforded to your estate can often be extended to include the assets in your living trust.

A Will Is Still Required

Even where you believe that you have transferred all your assets to your living trust, the reality is that you should still make a last will. In practice, it is extremely difficult to ensure that you have transferred every single asset you own to your living trust. On top of this difficulty, there is always the possibility that you end up receiving an unexpected inheritance shortly before you pass away and that you simply don't get time to transfer it to your trust. For example, you and your spouse could be fatally injured in a car accident in circumstances where he or she dies some time before you. In which case, you could probably end up receiving your deceased spouse's estate. Of course, if you have not made a will, the rules of intestacy would apply to govern how those assets are distributed amongst your heirs.

As such, it is normally recommended that you make either a standard will or a will called a 'pour-over will'. A pour-over will is usually created to stand side-by-side with a living trust. It ensures that any assets that you have not expressly or properly transferred to your living trust will 'pour-over' into the trust on your death. Under the pour-over will, your living trust is appointed as the sole beneficiary of all your assets. In turn, the terms of your living trust set out how all the trust assets will be distributed – even those received under your pour-over will. Assets received from your estate under a pour-over will tend to end up being gifted to the persons entitled to the benefit of the residuary trust estate. More on this later.

Of course, there are other important reasons for making a will. For example, a will presents an excellent opportunity to nominate guardians for your minor children. It also allows you to appoint an executor to wind up your estate and deal with any related matters following your death including dealing with taxes owing by your estate or litigation against it.

Capable of Being Challenged

Fortunately, while the likelihood of a will contest occurring is rare at best, the likelihood of someone challenging your living trust is even less due to the privacy surrounding its terms. However, while this is so, the chance of someone contesting the terms of your trust is by no means non-existent. An unhappy beneficiary could challenge a living trust in much the same way as a will based on grounds of capacity, fraud, undue influence, etc. If you believe there is a possibility that the terms of your living trust could be challenged, speak to your attorney.

CHAPTER 5

Types of Living Trusts

Types of Living Trust

There are two main types of living trusts used for estate planning purposes - namely basic living trusts and AB living trusts. A basic living trust, which can be used by an individual or a couple, has the primary objective of avoiding probate. An AB living trust, on the other hand, goes one step further by 'saving' on estate taxes as well as avoiding probate. Each of these types of trust is discussed in more detail below.

Living Trust for an Individual

If you're single, your primary objective in setting up a living trust will probably be to transfer your property to your loved ones after you die in a way that avoids the costs and delays often associated with probate. If this is the case, then a basic living trust could be right for you.

To create a basic living trust, all you need to do is sign a trust agreement. That agreement will be between you as 'grantor' and you as 'trustee'. Under the terms of the trust agreement, you will nominate someone to act as your successor trustee and set out the names of the people entitled to receive the trust's assets following your death. Once you have signed your trust agreement, the next step will be to transfer some or all your personal assets into the trust. To help you do this, we take a detailed look in Chapter 9 at the assets that you can transfer into your living trust and how to do so.

When you die, your successor trustee will step-in and assume control and management of the trust and its assets. He will then deal with the transfer of those assets to the beneficiaries named in the living trust agreement.

If you wish to leave gifts to your child or to a young beneficiary, you can use your living trust to do so. Under the trust agreement, you can create a sub-trust for the benefit of the relevant beneficiary and name the successor trustee as trustee of that trust. He will then manage the sub-trust assets on behalf of the beneficiary until the beneficiary is old enough to receive those assets in his own right. As an alternative, you could create a UTMA custodianship which operates in a similar way to a sub-trust. We discuss sub-trusts and custodianships further in Chapter 7.

Important Note

If you are a single parent with a minor child or children, you should create a will to appoint a testamentary guardian to care for them following your death. You cannot appoint a guardian for your children under the terms of your living trust as most states do not allow this. One reason for this would appear to be that, as a matter of public policy, the legislators wish to ensure that court judges have the last say in approving the appointment of guardians for minor children. Remember, with a living trust, you circumvent the court system as no probate is required. As such, the courts typically have no way of knowing that guardianship provisions have in fact been made.

Living Trusts for Couples

Spouses and partners tend to own property with each other as well as in their own individual names. As such, each spouse and partner will have the choice of creating two types of trust. Firstly, he or she can create an individual trust just for himself or herself. This will usually only include his/her own personal assets or 'separate property' as it is sometimes referred to. Alternatively, the spouses or partners can create a shared living trust with each other. This type of trust can hold both separate property and jointly held property that the couple owns together.

Did You Know

Separate property is property that a person owns absolutely in his own right. Joint, co-owned or community property is property that a person owns with another. This is not limited to real estate and can include personal property also. For example, it can include bank accounts, artwork, cars, and so on.

If you are married or in a registered domestic partnership, the state in which you live will have an impact on whether you can classify certain assets as separate property of jointly held property. For example, if you are resident in a community property state, it may be that a large part of your property is jointly held property. By contrast, if you are living in a common law state, the opposite may be true. We discussed some of the principal differences between these types of ownership in Chapter 2. You will recall that, depending on the state in which you are living, the law will determine what amounts to your individual property and what amounts to joint marital property.

Turning back to living trusts, there are four principal types of living trust arrangement that a couple can create including the following: -

(i)   Each spouse or partner can create their own individual basic living trust.

(ii)   Both spouses or partners can create a shared or joint basic living trust.

(iii)   Each spouses or partner can create a shared living trust with AB provisions, possibly with disclaimers.

(iv)   Both spouses and partners can create an AB living trust, possibly with disclaimers.

Each of these types of living trust is discussed in the ensuing pages. For convenience, when we speak of couples, we will refer only to spouses. However, the references should apply equally to couples in a registered domestic partnership.

Individual Living Trusts

There are many reasons why each spouse might want to create a separate individual trust for his or her own assets as opposed to creating a joint or shared living trust for all the couple's combined assets. For example, the use of individual trusts can make a lot of sense where spouses own most of their property separately rather than jointly. In which case, each spouse may wish to ensure that the other does not gain control over their assets once they have been transferred into a living trust. At the same time, each spouse may still want to avoid having their assets tied up in probate. An individual trust can be ideal in such circumstances.

However, there are drawbacks to spouses using individual trusts particularly when it comes to dealing with jointly held assets. The difficulty sometimes arises in the context of 'funding' the trusts. In the case of shared assets, financial institutions are generally reluctant to allow assets over which they have security (such as real estate) to be held jointly by a person and a living trust, or by two living trusts. As such, it can be difficult for an individual spouse to transfer their interest in a jointly held asset into their living trust. For this very reason, it can sometimes make sense to create another trust to hold only the couple's jointly held assets.

It is often recommended that couples use individual trusts, rather than a shared living trust, to deal with separately owned property and a separate shared living trust to deal with their jointly owned property. However, whether that is suitable in any given situation really depends on the nature and ownership of the assets that the couple intends to transfer into the trusts.

Basic Shared Living Trusts

While a couple may opt for individual trusts for personal reasons, for many married (and some unmarried) couples it often makes sense to create one basic shared living trust to hold both co-owned property and property that is separately owned.

Important Note

In the absence of a couple being married or in a registered domestic relationship, they should at least consider using individual trusts rather than a shared trust especially if they do not have co-owned property. Shared trusts are often more suitable for use with co-owned property.

As the trust is established by both spouses, both will act as co-grantors and co-trustees of the trust. As co-grantors, each spouse can nominate beneficiaries for their individual property, as well as for their portion of the jointly held property in the trust. In addition, each spouse has the power (exercisable at any time) to call for the return of his or her assets to him/her and to revoke the trust. When the trust is revoked, the trust assets must be returned to the spouse that placed them into the trust in the first place.

For so long as the trust remains in existence, each spouse retains control over the assets that he or she has placed into the trust – including both separate property and his or her share of jointly owned property. As both spouses have, in their capacity as trustees, control over the trust assets, third parties (such as banks and other financial institutions) dealing with the trust will normally require the signatures of both trustees before dealing with the trust property. This gives each grantor comfort that the other will not 'run off' with their assets.

When one of the spouses dies, the trust automatically splits into two separate trusts – the 'First Trust' and the 'Second Trust'. The deceased spouse's separate property and his/her share of the joint property automatically transfers to the First Trust. The remaining trust assets are automatically transferred to the Second Trust.

The terms of the trust agreement relating to the First Trust immediately become irrevocable on the death of the first spouse. This means that the surviving spouse cannot amend those terms in any way. The surviving spouse will be required, in his or her capacity as successor trustee, to distribute the deceased spouse's share of the trust property in accordance with the terms of the trust agreement. Of course, as most co-grantors are either married or in a relationship, it will come as no surprise that all or at least a large proportion of the deceased spouse's trust property is often left to the surviving spouse's Second Trust. In which case, there is often no need to transfer some or all the deceased spouse's trust property out of the trust. That said, each spouse is generally free to distribute or gift a large part of their property as they see fit - subject to any restrictions which apply in relation to the disinheritance of spouses generally. So, external transfers of assets are often carried out.

Important Note

If you are planning on establishing a shared trust in circumstances where one of the spouses will not act as a trustee of the trust, for whatever reason, we recommend that you consult with a lawyer before creating the trust and/or transferring any assets to it. This is especially so if you are the spouse that does not plan on becoming a trustee.

Once the Second Trust has been created, it will continue to exist as a standalone trust – like an individual trust. This trust will be capable of being revoked by the surviving spouse at any time in the same way that the grantor of an individual trust would be able to do so. When the surviving spouse ultimately dies, the trust assets will be distributed to the beneficiaries named in the trust agreement in the usual way.

Basic AB Trusts

Most people do not need to think about federal estate tax because it only affects those with large estates. But if you (or you and your spouse) expect that the value of your estate will exceed your unified tax credit (i.e. $ 11.7 million in 2021) then an AB trust could be a good idea for you. To understand AB trusts, it is important to first briefly look at the current estate tax laws.

As of 2021, the federal estate tax law provides that no estate tax will be assessed on a person's estate if the value of his or her estate at the time of death, plus the value large gifts made during his or her lifetime, was worth less than $11.7 million. This $11.7 million is referred to as the unified tax credit. The amount of the unified tax credit changes from year to year, and historic rates for the last 3 years are set out below.

Year of Death	Amount Exempt from Tax
2019	$ 11,400,000
2020	$11,580,000
2021	$11,700,000

Normally, a spouse leaves their entire estate to their spouse on death, partly for sentimental reasons and partly because the transfer is tax free due to the 'unlimited marital deduction' for estate taxes. This unlimited marital deduction allows spouses to gift assets to each other free from tax. However, while the gift was tax free, prior to 2009 (when the tax exemption was much lower at $3.5m) it was often only a waiting game as tax would most likely become payable on the death of the second spouse. This was particularly so when the value of a surviving spouse's enlarged estate, taking into account the value of their original estate and that received from their deceased spouse, exceeds their individual estate tax exemption threshold (i.e. the unified tax credit). If it did, the surplus would have been charged to estate tax, which is currently at 40% but which has been as high as 55% in recent years.

To reduce this tax burden, AB trusts were often used prior to 2011 because they enabled spouses to maximize the use of their respective unified tax credits to help avoid a charge to estate tax when the second spouse died. The precise manner in which AB trusts work will be explained in more detail below but in brief they allowed surviving spouses to use their deceased spouse's available tax credit as well as their own to increase their unified tax credit.

Following the introduction of changes to the federal estate tax regime in 2011, the use of AB trusts was called into question as a means of effectively reducing charges to estate taxes. The new laws provided that, for deaths occurring in 2011 and beyond, a surviving spouse may be able to add their deceased spouse's unused estate tax exemption to their own estate tax exemption. This could give him or her a possible exemption amount of $23.4 million ($11.7 million x 2) - thereby achieving the same result that AB trusts sought to achieve but without the need to create an AB trust – if neither spouse used up any of their exemption amounts by making gifts to others during their lifetimes.

The ability to transfer estate tax exemptions between spouses in this way is commonly referred to as "portability". To take advantage of portability, an estate tax return must be filed for the deceased spouse, even if no estate tax is due. However, the amount of estate tax exemption available under portability is limited to the unused exemption of the surviving spouse's most recently deceased spouse. So, he or she cannot, for example, use his or her first spouse's exemption if they later remarried.

As the future availability of portability hinges on so many factors that a deceased spouse cannot control during his or her lifetime, and as a number of states still charge separate estate taxes in addition to federal estate taxes, many people may still choose to use AB trusts in order to avoid the risk of the unused tax exemption of the first spouse going to waste.

Did You Know

AB trusts are designed for couples who (i) have a combined probate estate that is worth more than the current estate tax threshold and (ii) want to leave most, or all, of their respective property to the other.

While AB trusts have allowed married couples to reduce and even eliminate estate taxes since the early 1960s, the fact that the estate tax exemption for a single person has risen to $11.7 million in 2021 and that spouses can now avail of portability means that for most people, AB trusts will provide limited tax advantages going forward. That said, many people may still want to err on the side of caution (given the flexibility of revocable living trusts) and put a trust in place as the advantages of having that trust might far outweigh the disadvantages – particularly if portability was unavailable for some reason, including due to a change in tax laws.

How Does an AB Living Trust Work?

To illustrate how AB trusts work, it is useful to look at an example that ignores portability (although it may apply in practice). For the purposes of this example, let us assume that a husband and wife have a combined estate worth of $20 million with the husband and wife each individually owning $10 million worth of that estate.

In this case, each spouse could transfer their $10 million to their children without triggering a charge to estate tax – as each amount would be under the estate tax threshold. However, for many reasons, spouses tend not to transfer their assets directly to their children on their death but rather avail of their ability to transfer their estate to the other spouse tax free. Thereafter, the surviving spouse can have full use and ownership of the deceased spouse's assets. In time, the surviving spouse often ends up transferring all his or her assets to his or her children on death. The problem that this causes is that, at the time of this transfer, the 'surviving' spouse's estate may be worth more than the estate tax exemption – i.e. $11.7 million. In which case, the excess is charged to estate tax at the rate of 40%. This can and does have an enormous effect on the value of the estate that the beneficiaries receive.

The problem can, however, be avoided by creating an AB trust under the terms of your living trust (or in your last will). An AB trust works a little like a shared trust. When the first spouse dies, the trust property is split into two separate trusts – 'Trust A' and 'Trust B'. Trust A is the deceased spouse's trust which becomes irrevocable on his/her death and cannot be amended. Trust B, on the other hand, is the surviving spouse's trust which is revocable in the usual way.

Did You Know

What are AB trusts?

An AB trust is a trust that splits into two separate trusts upon the death of one of the grantors. One trust is called a 'Credit Shelter Trust' because it is designed to hold an amount of the grantor's property up to the value of the federal estate tax exemption threshold - $11.7 million for the tax year 2021. In this way, that amount does not become subject to tax because it is less than the taxable threshold. The other trust is called a Marital Trust because it is designed to hold the remainder of the deceased grantor's property which is sheltered from the federal estate tax by virtue of the unlimited marital deduction. These trusts serve to reduce and/or eliminate the liability to federal estate tax which could otherwise be incurred by a married couple over the deaths of both spouses.

Immediately upon the creation of the two trusts, assets equal to the value of the estate tax threshold amount are transferred to the deceased spouse's Trust A for the benefit of the beneficiaries - usually his or her children. The balance of the assets will be transferred to Trust B.

The terms of the AB trust agreement will normally provide that the surviving spouse will have a lifetime interest in the assets transferred to Trust A. This means that, while the assets are being held for the benefit of certain named beneficiaries, for so long as the surviving spouse is alive, he or she will have the use and benefit of the assets in Trust A. The surviving spouse can therefore use all the income generated from the property in Trust A for his or her own support and upkeep but will not own that property. As he or she does not own the property, the surviving spouse cannot simply sell those assets or give them away. Of course, if the surviving spouse is also the trustee of Trust A, he or she may have a power to sell the property on behalf of the trust and keep the proceeds in the trust.

When the surviving spouse dies, all the trust property in both Trust A and Trust B is distributed to the beneficiaries in accordance with the terms of the AB trust agreement. As the deceased spouse's share of the Trust A property was never transferred to the surviving spouse, the deceased spouse is still able to avail of the $11.7 million estate tax exemption in relation to transfers from his or her estate – which will of course be taking place sometime after his or her death. As such, the deceased spouse's $10 million sitting in Trust A can be passed on to the beneficiaries named in the AB trust agreement tax-free. Similarly, the 'surviving' spouse's (who is of course now deceased) $10 million can also be transferred tax free to his or her beneficiaries as named in the trust agreement. This, in essence, means that the beneficiaries, who are most likely the children of the couple, can receive a combined amount of up to $23.4 million tax-free from the spouses – an amount which is far in excess of the amount which they would have received under the terms of a will or an ordinary living trust had no tax planning measures been employed or had portability not been used.

Important Note

It is also possible to create trusts and provide for life interests under the terms of a last will and testament such that the same tax treatment is obtained as that received from a living trust. A discussion of this mechanism is, however, beyond the scope of this book.

Disadvantages of an AB Living Trust

Despite the clear benefits, there are also several disadvantages associated with the use of AB living trusts. These include:

(i)   The use of the trust property by the surviving spouse may be restricted. The rights of the surviving spouse to deal with the trust property must be limited to ensure that the value of the trust property does not accidentally become included in the surviving spouse's estate. For example, the surviving spouse may be entitled only to the income produced by the trust property. If the spouse is entitled to principle of the trust, there must be limits placed on the ways in which the spouse can access the trust property. For example, the principal in Trust A will not usually be deemed to form part of the surviving spouse's estate if he or she is permitted to use the trust property only for his or her health, education, support and maintenance.

(ii) The spouses may need to pay legal or accounting fees to facilitate the division of property between Trust A and Trust B.

(iii) Tax returns must be filed on behalf of both Trust A and Trust B.

(iv) Separate records must be kept regarding the trust property in each of the two trusts.

(v)   The irrevocable nature of Trust A makes it less suitable in cases where one spouse is a good deal younger than the other or where the couple is quite young. In those instances, any tax benefits will have to be weighed against the disadvantages of locking up a certain element of the estate in an irrevocable trust.

AB Disclaimer Trust

An AB disclaimer trust works the same as the basic AB trust, apart from one important factor – the right of the surviving spouse to determine how much, if any, property goes into Trust A.

An AB disclaimer trust is a trust that names the surviving spouse as the beneficiary of the other spouse's estate (which is tax free in the normal course). However, on the death of the first spouse, the surviving spouse has the option of renouncing or disclaiming all or part of the trust assets which he or she is to receive from the deceased spouse if the combined value of their estates exceeds the estate tax exemption threshold amount at the time of the first spouse's death. The disclaimed assets would pass to a credit shelter trust (like Trust A for the Basic AB trust discussed above) for the benefit of the surviving spouse – who will have a life interest in these trust assets.

Apart from that one specific point in respect of disclaimers, both trusts are quite similar. In fact, like the situation with basic AB trusts, the assets in both Trust A and Trust B will be distributed on the death of the surviving spouse.

Conclusion

You should carefully consider the use of each of the above types of trust before deciding that any of them would suit your circumstances. Remember, as well as the advantages, there are several drawbacks to using the different types of living trust. If you are in any doubt as to the type of trust which is most suitable to your circumstances, you should consult a qualified and experienced estate planning attorney.

Caution

Remember to read a trust agreement in its entirety before signing it. There are lots of different agreements available online and not all of them say the same thing or are drafted with a high degree of care and diligence.

CHAPTER 6

Trustees & Successor Trustees

The Role of the Initial Trustee

A trustee is a person appointed under the terms of a trust agreement or deed to manage trust assets on behalf of one or more persons in accordance with the terms of that trust document. As well as managing the trust assets, the trustee will also be charged with the task of administering the trust generally.

In the case of living trusts, the grantor or creator of the trust usually appoints himself as the initial trustee of the trust. Where there are two grantors, such as in the case of a shared or joint living trust, both grantors are usually appointed as co-trustees. This appointment of the grantor as trustee is a key feature of revocable living trusts as the principal purpose behind the use of these trusts is to bypass probate in a way that allows the grantor to retain control over his or her assets.

You may of course decide, either at the time you create your living trust or at a later date, that you would prefer to nominate someone else to act as trustee of your living trust instead of you. That is perfectly fine. The new trustee will be obliged to act in accordance with your instructions as grantor of the trust – provided of course that those instructions are legal. However, before you make that appointment, you should speak to your attorney. The appointment of a new trustee in this manner will result in you losing day-to-day control of the trust assets. This could have significant legal and practical consequences for you, and you will need to understand those before deciding. In addition, if you appoint a trustee other than yourself, you will need to obtain a tax identification number for your trust from the Internal Revenue Service (IRS) and ensure that your trustee makes income tax returns on behalf of the trust.

However, from a practical perspective, given that you were able to manage your assets and affairs while the assets were in your personal name, there should be no reason why you can't manage them in your capacity as trustee of the living trust after they have been transferred to it. The reality is that, as trustee of your own revocable living trust, you do not really owe too many duties to people other than yourself (as grantor). As such, you can often simply carry on managing your affairs as you always have provided you do not breach the terms of the trust agreement.

For so long as you are the sole trustee of your living trust, or you and your spouse are in the case of a shared living trust, you should not need to file any special tax returns on behalf of the trust itself. You simply report any income the trust property generates with your own income tax returns in the same way that you always did (or, at least, should have done).

Appointing a Co-Trustee

If you so wish, rather than hand over the management of your trust assets to another person entirely, you could simply engage someone to assist you in the management of your trust property. You can do this quite easily by appointing someone as a co-trustee of your living trust. As co-trustees, both of you would have authority to act on the trust's behalf. While there is no real difficulty with having someone else act as trustee of your trust or even having someone act as a co-trustee, we recommend that you speak to a lawyer before you do this as the terms of your trust document may need to be tailored to cater for this eventuality.

Important Note

Instead of appointing a co-trustee, you could also appoint someone as a property manager or advisor to help you manage your trust assets. As this person would not be a co-trustee, you would not have to cede any real control to him or her.

Appointing a Successor Trustee

As mentioned, your successor trustee is the person who will assume control of your living trust after you become incapacitated or die. In the case of a shared or joint trust, the successor trustee will take over control of the trust when both trustees have become incapacitated or have died. The successor trustee will have no authority to act while any of the grantors remain alive and capable of managing the trust. Your trust agreement will identify the person or persons who will act as successor trustee(s) of your trust. In most cases, this is usually a capable relative or family friend.

Important Note

One of the most important choices that you will make in relation to your living trust will be your choice of successor trustee(s). Be careful about choosing a trustee simply because he or she is a family member or close friend. Choose someone you implicitly trust, someone that is competent and capable of handling the demands of a successor trustee's role.

If your living trust is relatively straightforward and the trust assets do not require a significant degree of management, you have a little more flexibility in terms of who you can choose as a successor trustee. However, if there are sub-trusts created for the benefit of young beneficiaries or assets that require close and careful management, you should choose a successor trustee who has the requisite skills to deal with these.

Of course, as well as choosing someone with the relevant skills, you also need to choose someone who is honestly willing to do the job for you. There is little point in having to pressure someone into taking on the role. They need to be happy and ready to accept the task, and if they are not, you should consider someone else.

It is important to bear in mind that even though you nominate and appoint someone to act as your successor trustee in your trust agreement, he or she is under absolutely no obligation to take on the role and cannot be forced to do so. In fact, it is open to anyone named as a successor trustee to decline to act. Where this happens, the alternate successor trustee you named in your trust agreement will be asked to take on the role. If he or she is also unwilling to serve, the beneficiaries of the trust will need to petition the local court to have someone appointed to fulfill the role unless they have specific authority under the trust agreement to appoint a successor trustee themselves.

Even where a person takes on the role as successor trustee, he or she may choose to resign at any point. However, the terms of a professionally written trust agreement will ensure that he or she cannot easily be relieved or replaced until a new successor trustee takes over. This is to ensure that the trust assets are not left unmanaged at any time.

Appointing an Alternate Successor Trustee

It is important that you name at least one alternate successor trustee in case your first chosen successor trustee is unable or unwilling to act when the time comes. Naturally if you named two, or even more, successor trustees, the alternate trustee would not become a trustee at all unless all your original choices are unable or unwilling to take on the role. If an alternate successor trustee is required to act, he or she will be bound by the same fiduciary duties and responsibilities as the original successor trustee(s). The fiduciary duties of trustees are discussed further in the ensuing pages.

It is often useful to include a clause in a living trust agreement that allows someone, such as the largest beneficiary of the trust, to appoint a successor trustee of their choosing if none of the successor trustees or alternates named in the trust document are able and willing to act. This type of clause removes the need to make a court application to appoint a successor trustee where none of the named successor trustees are able or willing to act.

The Role of the Successor Trustee

Most successor trustees will have two specific roles. The first is to manage and administer the trust during any periods in which the primary trustee (i.e. the grantor) is incapacitated and unable to manage the trust himself. The second arises on the death of the grantor, in which case the successor trustee steps in to distribute the trust assets and wind up the trust estate. Responsibilities and obligations are placed on successor trustees in each situation. We look at these in more detail below.

Role of a Successor Trustee if the Grantor Becomes Incapacitated

If it is suspected that the grantor is incapacitated, the first thing that the successor trustee will need to do is locate the living trust agreement. Normally, a living trust agreement will contain a clear set of instructions for determining whether the grantor is in fact incapacitated. This usually requires one or sometimes two doctors to certify in writing that the grantor is unable to manage his or her affairs. If the doctors certify that to be the case, the successor trustee will be able to step-in and take control of the trust property.

Once he steps in, one of the first duties of the successor trustee will be to ensure that you (the grantor) are in receipt of appropriate medical care and attention. In this regard, he will need to review the terms of your living trust. Usually, the terms of a living trust will allow for the successor trustee to apply an element of the trust property towards the provision of medical care to the grantor. In some cases, this will only be permitted after the grantor's personal assets (i.e. those sitting outside the living trust) and insurance policies are first used. The successor trustee will need to work closely with your family and any agent named in a durable power of attorney to determine the exact position in this respect. This is particularly so because financial institutions may not deal with the successor trustee in respect of assets sitting outside of the living trust, such as medical insurance policies.

In any event, as a matter of prudence, your successor trustee should locate and familiarize himself with your insurance coverage (medical and long-term care, if any) and understand the associated benefits and limitations. For this reason, you should consider letting him have details of this coverage. Should the need for a claim arise, the successor trustee may need to ensure that the insurance company is notified of your illness and ensure that a claim is made (most likely by your family) in due course.

If you have any children or dependents, the successor trustee may also need to arrange for their care. While your successor trustee will be limited in terms of what he can do in respect of their physical care, he will often have authority to apply trust funds towards the welfare, care and education of your children and dependents.

Your successor trustee should also get familiar with your finances, the location of your assets and the sources of your income. If there is not a detailed schedule of the trust assets attached to your living trust agreement (which there should be), your successor trustee may need to contact various parties connected to you in order to determine the specific assets that you have transferred into your living trust and the extent of your assets and income generally. More specifically, he may need to contact your family, financial and legal advisors, tax advisor, employer, accountant, etc. to get to the bottom of your affairs. Remember, he needs to understand whether you have sufficient resources to pay for your medical care or whether the trust needs to sell some assets to finance this care. He will also need to manage your assets to ensure that their value is preserved in so far as is possible in the circumstances.

If your successor trustee needs to communicate with any financial institutions or third parties, he will most likely need to provide them with a copy of the doctors' certificate(s) of incapacity as well as a copy of your living trust document. These parties will want to see both documents before dealing with him. In certain cases, financial institutions may ask for a certificate from the successor trustee (instead of a full copy of the living trust agreement) to show that he has been validly appointed under the terms of the living trust agreement before dealing with him. The lawyer who drafted the trust should be able to prepare this certificate if required. Alternatively, a sample certificate is contained at the back of this book, albeit for use with the living trust agreements that are also included. That said, you could modify the certificate to reflect the terms of any other living trust you have made.

Also, if there are expenses to be paid, the successor trustee may need to discharge them from the trust fund. The successor trustee will need to keep records of all money paid into the trust and all disbursements made from the trust during any period in which he is acting on behalf of the trust. In fact, he may even be required under the terms of the trust agreement to send a copy of the trust accounts to the beneficiaries of the trust.

Finally, the successor trustee will also need to file income tax returns for the trust in respect of the period in which he is managing the trust. We discussed this briefly in previous pages.

If you recover from your incapacity, everything goes back to normal and the successor trustee will no longer need to act on your behalf. You should however request a copy of the ledger or trust accounts from the successor trustee so that you can review the transactions that took place during the period in which you were incapacitated. If there any irregularities, the successor trustee may be held accountable.

Role of a Successor Trustee After the Grantor Dies

After you die, the role assumed by your successor trustee will be quite like that of a typical executor of an estate. One of the major differences, however, will be that your successor trustee will not be subject to any court supervision. Instead, he will be subject only to the requirements of your trust agreement and the laws applicable to trustees. Subject to complying with these provisions and laws, he will be responsible for the payment of bills, the location, collection and management of the trust assets and the subsequent distribution of those trust assets to the beneficiaries named in your living trust agreement. We review this entire process in detail in Chapter 11.

Payment of Compensation to Successor Trustees

Trustees are generally entitled to be paid reasonable compensation for carrying out their duties as trustee. The amount of this compensation will normally be set out in the trust document. If it is not, state law often sets out the level of fees that ought to be paid to a trustee in such circumstances. In order to avoid paying large fees to successor trustees or even to reduce the amount that may need to be paid to them, grantors often choose a family member or a close friend to act as their successor trustee. These people are likely to see their selection as an honor and are therefore not likely to charge for providing their services or, at the least, they will charge modestly.

Entitlement to Act as a Successor Trustee

In most states, you can appoint an individual who has reached the age of 18 years as a successor trustee - provided he has not been convicted of a felony. This individual could even be a beneficiary under your living trust. In addition, you can also appoint a corporate body to act as your successor trustee. In fact, most professional trustees are corporate bodies. You should be aware, however, that professional trustees usually charge a pretty penny for providing their services.

Important Note

Remember, before appointing someone as a successor trustee, ask them whether they would be happy to accept the role in the first place. There is no benefit in appointing someone who is likely to refuse the position when the time comes.

Remember also that you can appoint one or more successor trustees. You can even appoint one or more alternate successor trustees in case your primary successor trustees are unwilling or unable to take on the role when the time comes.

Whom Should You Choose as a Successor Trustee?

A trustee's duties can continue for a number of years and, in many cases, require expertise in investing money, dealing with real estate, paying bills, filing accounts, and managing money on behalf of the trust's underlying beneficiaries.

One of the biggest decisions that you will need to make when deciding on who to appoint as your successor trustee will be whether to appoint a family member, a professional trustee or both. In practice most people who set up a living trust appoint family members. This is fine so long as the family member can handle the financial matters involved and has sufficient time to carry out his or her role – and of course is willing to do so. You should also bear in mind that individual trustees are generally entitled to engage the services of professional advisors if required. The fees associated with such appointments will be borne by the trust itself rather than the successor trustee.

Professional trustees will charge annual management fees for acting as trustees. In some instances, these fees can be significant. However, given the expertise that a professional trustee can bring to the table, it is important to at least consider engaging a professional where you have a large trust estate.

If you decide not to proceed with appointing a professional, then the characteristics you should consider in appointing a trustee are good common sense, excellent organizational skills, and integrity. Some people choose to appoint their spouse, a sibling, or an adult child, while others prefer to nominate a professional such as a lawyer or accountant. Alternatively, it can simply be a good friend. Whoever you choose should be both competent and trustworthy.

It may also make sense to appoint someone who is living nearby as successor trustee so that he will be well placed to deal with the management, collection, and distribution of the trust assets.

Your successor trustee must be willing and prepared to carry out all the legal steps required to finalize the distribution of the trust assets and the wind up of the trust itself. As such, you should always consult your choice of successor trustee before you sign your trust agreement to ensure that he would be happy to take on the role.

If the job is likely to be a sizeable one, it is common for successor trustees to be paid fees out of the trust assets to compensate them for their services. Trustee fees are often statutorily limited to a percentage of the trust's value or to 'reasonable compensation'. However, often only professional trustees require such payment.

Successor Trustee's Duties

Successor trustees, like other trustees, have many duties which vary from state to state. A trustee occupies a fiduciary position (a position of trust) and is therefore bound to act for the benefit of and in the best interests of another. Some specific duties that trustees tend to have (depending on state law) include the following:

The Duty to Adhere to the Terms of the Trust

Trustees are required to administer a trust according to its terms. Surprisingly, however, many trustees make decisions without referring to the trust provisions to establish whether the act in question is permitted under the terms of the trust. Where the trustee's decisions are outside of what is permitted under the trust rules and have an adverse effect on the value of the underlying trust assets, the trustee can be exposed to personal liability for the losses incurred. A prudent successor trustee should always commence his role by carefully reading the terms of the trust document to understand the scope of the duties assigned to him and to determine what immediate actions he must take.

The Duty to Secure Assets

A successor trustee should immediately determine what assets are currently in the trust and what assets might be added to the trust (i) under any probate proceedings taking place in relation to the grantor's estate and (ii) from payments receivable under the grantor's insurance policies or retirement plans. He should also ensure that the assets contained in the trust are registered in the name of the trust and that he is authorized to deal with those assets in his capacity as successor trustee of the living trust. Simultaneously with this, the successor trustee should also locate and secure all the trust assets. If real estate or other valuables need to be insured or secured for a period, he will need to arrange this. If accounts need to be changed into the trust's name, again this should be arranged.

The Duty to Act Personally

Unless the trust terms permit otherwise, trustees must act personally and may not delegate the performance of tasks or the making of decisions concerning the trust to others – although the trustee is normally permitted to take legal and other professional advice when necessary.

The Duty to Act in the Best Interests of the Beneficiaries

The trustee is required to act impartially and in the best interest of the trust's beneficiaries. If he does not, a beneficiary can apply to the court to have him removed or to have his decision reviewed or reversed.

The Duty to Account

A trustee is required to maintain detailed records of all transactions carried out by him in relation to the trust estate and its assets. In particular, a trustee is obliged to keep detailed records of income generated by the trust assets, any sale or purchase of trust assets and any payments made using trust assets including all payments of taxes and debts and all distributions made to beneficiaries. From time to time, a trustee may be required to provide a copy of those records to the beneficiaries of the trust. Normally, this accounting will take place on an annual basis. However, it will not be required where the terms of the trust document expressly provide otherwise.

An annual accounting typically includes some or all the following:

(i)   a statement of the trust's income and expenditure.

(ii)   a statement of the trust's assets and liabilities.

(iii)   details of the successor trustee's compensation for the accounting period in question.

(iv)   (in some states) a notification to the beneficiaries that they are entitled to petition the court for a review of the acts of the successor trustee (including his accounting).

(v)   (in some states) a statement that all beneficiaries have a period of three years within which they can take a claim against the successor trustee for wrongdoings.

The Duty to Supply Information

A trust's beneficiaries may be entitled to certain information regarding the trust after you die. While the terms of your trust agreement may specify the precise information to which your beneficiaries are entitled, they are typically entitled to a copy of the trust deed, latest financial accounts, copies of title documents relating to the trust assets and details of any distributions made from the trust to beneficiaries. However, trustees are not normally required to provide explanations for their decisions, minutes of trustee meetings (if any), copies of correspondence between trustees and other beneficiaries, nor are they required to provide any memorandum of wishes provided by the grantor.

Several states also require successor trustees to notify the beneficiaries of a trust once the trust has become irrevocable. This of course usually only happens when a grantor or co-grantor of a trust dies. This notice, the terms of which are usually set out under state law, advises beneficiaries that they have a certain period of time (such as 120 days) to contest the legitimacy and standing of the trust and that they may request a copy of the trust documents and any amendments made to it. If a successor trustee fails to serve this notice, he may be liable for fines or otherwise.

The Duty to Invest Prudently

State laws typically provide that a trustee must exercise the same due care, diligence, and skill in managing the trust assets that would be expected from a prudent person carrying on the same task. For example, the California Uniform Prudent Investor Act requires that trustees "shall invest and manage trust assets as a prudent investor would, by considering the purpose, terms, distribution requirements, and other circumstances of the trust". It follows that a trustee will need to diversify the trust estate's investments to balance the potential risk of depletion in the value of those investments. In tandem with doing this, he also needs to ensure the generation of income from the trust assets while at the same time ensuring that the value of those assets grows. For these reasons, it is prudent for a successor trustee (who will often have little investment experience) to engage the services of an investment advisor who can provide investment advice and guidance to him. The appointment of such an advisor becomes more prudent when account is taken of the fact that any failure by the successor trustee to act diligently and prudently in the management of the trust's assets could result in the beneficiaries suing him personally for any depletion in the value of those assets. However, if the successor trustee acts prudently, it is unlikely that he could be sued even where the value of the estate assets is reduced.

The Duty to Carry Out Duties Without Payment

Except for out of pocket expenses, trustees are generally required to act without payment unless the trust terms provide otherwise. Professional trustees will always ensure that a power to pay them is contained within the trust document before they act.

The Duty to Not Benefit Personally from the Trust

As a fiduciary, that is a person occupying a position of trust regarding someone else's assets, a trustee may not benefit personally from his role unless the trust document specifically allows for this.

The Duty to Avoid Conflicts of Interest

Trustees are required to act in good faith and to avoid conflicts of interest. When a conflict of interest arises, a successor trustee should act carefully and consider taking professional advice and/or disclosing the nature of his interest to the trust's beneficiaries.

Keeping Trust Assets Separate

A successor trustee should ensure that (i) the trust assets are kept wholly separate from both his own assets and third party assets, (ii) the title to each trust asset rests exclusively with the trust and not with the successor trustee personally, (iii) he accounts in full to the trust estate for all income generated by the trust's assets and (iv) he does not borrow or otherwise take money from the trust estate for his own benefit.

Paying Taxes, Claims and Expenses

When the grantor dies, the trust becomes irrevocable. This means that its terms cannot be changed and that no assets can be added to or taken out of the trust (save in the case of distributions made to the trust's beneficiaries). At this point, the trust's assets become subject to federal estate tax. The successor trustee must now carry out a valuation of all the trust's assets as at the date of death of the grantor and determine whether any federal estate tax is due. Remember, however, as the trust is essentially tax transparent, the determination of whether any federal tax is payable will also involve an assessment of the value of the assets held by the grantor outside of the trust. In this respect, a successor trustee should work closely with the executor of the grantor's estate, if any, and the trustee of any other trusts created by the grantor. If the combined total of the grantor's estate exceeds the unified tax credit ($11.7 million in 2021), then tax may need to be paid. For more information on tax, See Chapter 8.

In addition to the payment of taxes, the successor trustee, in much the same way as an executor, will need to deal with the payment of any outstanding debts owed by the trust as well as the settlement of any claims from creditors. Ordinarily, unless the estate is showing a large surplus of assets, all of this should be done before any distributions are made to the beneficiaries of the trust.

Making Payments from the Trust

The successor trustee may become obliged to make payments from the trust fund on the incapacity of the grantor and the death of the grantor. Dealing first with incapacity, a successor trustee can make discretionary payments for the "health, support, and welfare" of the grantor and, usually, for the benefit of the grantor's minor children and dependents. In making such payments, the trustee has a duty to act in the best interest of the trust and its beneficiaries (which includes the grantor during his or her lifetime). Following the death of the grantor, the successor trustee will be obliged to distribute the trust assets amongst the beneficiaries of the trust in accordance with the terms of the trust agreement. He cannot deviate from the express terms of the trust agreement when making any payments to the beneficiaries unless the terms of the trust agreement expressly permit him to do so.

Changing Trustees

The trust document should clearly provide that a successor trustee has the right to resign from office at any time. The simple reality is that you cannot force someone to do something that he does not want to do. That said, while you may be happy to release a successor trustee from office, you will want to ensure that in doing so there is an orderly transition of management and control from that person to the replacement successor trustee. To facilitate this transition, you may want to get an accounting of the trust property from the resigning successor trustee and to ensure that in the run up to his resignation date, he discharges certain bills, makes certain payments to beneficiaries and makes any critical investment decisions that may need to be made. In order words, you do not want him to become complacent.

It is generally advisable to require a successor trustee to give between 14 to 30 days' notice of his intended resignation to you if you are still living or to the trust's beneficiaries if you are already dead at the time the notice is served. If any of the trust's beneficiaries are minors, that notice should be served on that beneficiary's guardians. These notice requirements will ensure that you or the beneficiaries of the trust have sufficient time to have a successor trustee in place before the resigning trustee resigns.

Another thing that should be considered when changing successor trustees is the whole issue of confidentiality. The resigning successor trustee will be privy to private information about the trust, its assets, and its beneficiaries. It might therefore be advisable to consider having the successor trustee sign some form of confidentiality agreement or non-disclosure agreement when he resigns.

Removing a Trustee

The trust document should provide that you, as the creator of the trust, have the right to remove a successor trustee at your absolute discretion and without cause. After all, it is your trust.

If a beneficiary of your trust, on the other hand, is either unhappy or concerned about the manner in which a successor trustee is dealing with the trust property while you are incapacitated or after you die, and the situation cannot be resolved by discussion between them, he or she will have the option of petitioning the court to effect the removal of the successor trustee. However, in the absence of just cause, the beneficiary will find it extremely difficult to remove the successor trustee.

Conclusion

A successor trustee occupies a position of immense trust and one that requires a high degree of attention to detail and diligence. He must read and understand the terms of the trust document under which he is appointed and from which his authority stems. It is only with this understanding that he can carry out his role with due care and skill. If the successor trustee acts in breach of provisions of the trust agreement or in a manner which is not in the best interest of the beneficiaries, whether innocently or recklessly, he could well find himself the subject of a law suit in which he may be held personally liable for any loss caused to the trust estate.

To protect himself from such proceedings, the successor trustee will need to act diligently in accordance with the law and in the best interests of the trust. He will need to seek professional advice where he is in any doubt as to (i) what course of action he should take regarding the trust assets or any of its beneficiaries or (ii) how to interpret a provision of the trust deed or a provision of law. At every turn, he needs to be acting consciously and diligently.

CHAPTER 7

Making Gifts Under Your Living Trust

Types of Gifts

A gift is a voluntary transfer of property by one person to another made gratuitously, without any consideration or compensation. In your living trust, you may leave gifts of financial or personal value to your family and friends. Gifts can come in the form of specific item gifts, cash gifts or a gift of the residuary of your trust estate.

Important Note

When we use the term "gift" here, we are referring to gifts made by your living trust following your death – and not gifts made during your lifetime.

Specific Item Gifts

These gifts include specific items of property which you have transferred into your trust such as a car, a piece of jewelry, stocks, bonds, and real estate. When drafting your living trust, it is important to ensure that you clearly identify and describe the property that you wish to gift. For example, when gifting a car, you should describe the make, model, and color of the car rather than simply referring to "the car". This reduces the risk of confusion and accelerates the process of distributing the trust estate. When writing a provision for a gift, a good question to ask is whether a stranger would easily identify the gift based on the description you have included in your living trust.

Cash Gifts

A cash gift is a gift of a specific amount of money or cash to a named beneficiary. Just as with specific item gifts, when making a cash gift it is important to clearly identify the gift you are making including the amount and currency of the gift, and the person receiving the gift. In addition, when making a cash gift, it is important to consider the financial implications of the gift on the overall trust estate and, in particular, whether there will be enough cash remaining in the trust estate to pay any debts and taxes. If not, specific assets may need to be sold to raise cash.

Gift of the Residuary Trust Estate

The residue of your trust estate (or residuary trust estate, as it is often called) is the remainder of the trust assets in the trust after the payment of all debts and expenses and after all specific item gifts and cash gifts have been made. A residuary estate also includes property that is the subject of a failed gift. A gift fails in circumstances where the beneficiary has died before the gift is made or refuses their right to accept the gift. The person entitled to receive a gift of the residuary trust estate under your living trust is called the 'residuary beneficiary' or, if there is more than one beneficiary, 'residuary beneficiaries'.

What Is a Beneficiary?

A beneficiary is a person, organization or other entity who will inherit part of the trust assets under the terms of your living trust. In most cases, beneficiaries include spouses, children, siblings, relatives, friends, charities, and even local churches.

Some restrictions may be placed on minor beneficiaries, depending on the state in which the child is resident. Specifically, a child will be prohibited from owning significant assets until he has reached the age of majority in his state. Where a child is named as a beneficiary under a living trust, the assets gifted to the child will be placed in to the care of a trustee or guardian who will hold them in trust until such time as the child is old enough to take control of the assets in his own right. This trustee may or may not be your successor trustee.

Types of Beneficiaries

There are three principal types of beneficiaries under a living trust. These include a specific gift beneficiary, an alternate beneficiary, and a residuary beneficiary.

Specific Gift Beneficiary

A specific gift beneficiary is a person or organization named in your living trust to receive a specific item of property from your trust estate. These items of property tend to include items such as sums of money, jewelry, stocks, etc. Specific gifts are generally the first gifts distributed under the terms of a living trust. As mentioned above, any assets that are not distributed as specific gifts will form part of the residue of your trust estate and will usually be given (unless there are taxes or other expenses to be discharged) to the person or persons named as residuary beneficiaries.

Alternate Beneficiary

When naming a person to receive a specific gift or a gift of the residue of your trust estate under your living trust, it's prudent to prepare for the possibility that one or more of your beneficiaries will be unable or unwilling (for whatever reason) to accept the gift. To this end, it is helpful to nominate an alternate beneficiary. An alternate beneficiary is a person who becomes legally entitled to inherit the gift if the first named beneficiary is unable or unwilling to accept it. A beneficiary who refuses to accept a gift is said to have 'disclaimed' their entitlement to the gift in question. It is advisable to have all such disclaimers in writing before the gift is passed to the alternate beneficiary. Alternate beneficiaries are the second class of beneficiaries to inherit under your living trust.

Residuary Beneficiary

A residuary beneficiary is the person(s), or organization(s) named to receive the residue of the trust estate. The residue of a trust estate is that part of the estate which remains after the payment of all debts and expenses, and after the transfer of all specific gifts.

Gifts to Spouses

Before making a gift to your spouse, it is important to understand the basic differences in distribution of property in both common law property states and community property states. These differences will determine what portion of your estate (if any) you are obliged to transfer to your spouse.

Important Note

In this section, for convenience, we refer to 'spouses' only. However, the law tends to apply equally to registered domestic partners.

Community Property States

Property owned by couples in community property states is divided loosely into two categories: *separate property* and *community property*.

A spouse's *separate property* is all property acquired by that spouse before or after a marriage (including after a legal separation) plus all property received as a gift or an inheritance and maintained separately (not jointly owned with their spouse) during the marriage. *Community property*, on the other hand, is all other property earned or acquired by either spouse during a marriage.

Alaska, Arizona, California, Nevada, Texas and Wisconsin each allow a surviving spouse to automatically inherit community property when the other spouse dies provided that the property's title document makes it clear that it is owned as community property with a "right of survivorship" in favor of the surviving spouse.

Did You Know

At the date of writing, there are nine community property states: Arizona, California, Idaho, Louisiana, Nevada, New Mexico, Texas, Washington, and Wisconsin. In Alaska, couples can opt to have their property treated as community property under the terms of a written property agreement.

Separate property can also be deemed community property where it is formerly transferred to the joint names of both spouses. Similarly, where joint property is gifted to one spouse and commingled with community property, the property can become community property.

Normally, classifying property as community or separate property is relatively straightforward. However, there are several instances in which the classification is not clear. These include ownership of businesses, companies, and pensions, the proceeds of certain lawsuits, and incomes received from separate property. In each case, you should consult a local attorney to determine how the law in your state treats these items.

Most community property states do not grant a surviving spouse a legal right to inherit from the deceased spouse's estate. Rather, community property states try to divide the marital assets during the lifetime of the spouses by classifying certain assets as community property. Each spouse in turn has a right to 50% of the community property.

However, in Alaska, California, Idaho, Washington and Wisconsin, a surviving spouse may elect to receive a specific portion of the deceased spouse's community or separate property in limited circumstances. For more information on such entitlements, we recommend that you consult a suitably qualified attorney in your state.

Important Note

If you are married or in a registered domestic partnership and considering a move to another state, you should pay close attention to laws of the state to which you are proposing to move as the 'new state' may not recognize the same property rights which you had in your 'old state'. If you are in any doubt as to how the law will affect you, you should consult a duly qualified attorney in your state.

Common Law States

In common law states, each spouse owns all property acquired using his or her own income as well as all property legally registered solely in his or her name. In addition, each spouse will jointly own any property, such as the marital home, that is registered in the joint names of both spouses.

Spouses in common law states will also have a legal right, known as an elective share, to a fraction of their deceased spouse's estate when he or she dies. Depending on the state in which the couple are resident when the first spouse dies, this elective share will usually be an amount equal to between one-third and one-half of the value of the deceased spouse's estate. The precise amount to which the surviving spouse is entitled will also depend on whether the couple had any minor children and whether the surviving spouse had been provided for outside the terms of your living trust (for example, under a will).

The right of the surviving spouse to receive his or her elective share will take priority over any devises or legacies made in the deceased spouse's will or living trust, and will rank in priority after creditors of the deceased's estate. The surviving spouse is entitled to exercise his or her right to receive the elective share or to waive that right in favor of whatever has been left to him or her under the terms of the deceased spouse's will or living trust. The entitlement to receive an elective share does not arise by operation of law. Instead, the surviving spouse must exercise the right by serving a written notice on the executor of the deceased spouse's estate within a particular time frame. If the election is not made within the required time frame, the surviving spouse is deemed to have waived any entitlement to receive his or her elective share.

In certain states, the surviving spouse may have an additional right to inherit the family home or, in certain cases, a right to live there for a defined period. In some states, the surviving spouse will even be entitled to day-to-day living expenses during the probate process.

Matters can become more complex when a couple moves from a common law state to a community property state. In California, Idaho, Washington and Wisconsin, property acquired prior to a move will be treated as if it had been acquired in the state to which the couple has moved. In other community property states, the laws stipulate that the couple's property be treated in accordance with the laws of the state in which it was acquired rather those of the community property state to which the couple has moved. The application of these rules can result in marital property being subjected to both common law and community property rules. By contrast, couples that move from a community property state to a common law state come up against the opposite problem. In such cases, each spouse usually retains a 50% interest in the community property acquired during the couple's residence in the community property state.

It is important to determine which laws affect the distribution of your property before making your living trust. As such, be sure to take legal advice where necessary to determine the rules applicable - particularly where the rules of both community property states and common law states apply.

Gifts to Minors

Depending on each state's laws, minor children may only own a nominal amount of property in their own names, whether received under the terms of a living trust, a will or otherwise. The amount varies between approximately $1,000 and $5,000 depending on the state in question. If you plan on leaving a gift to a minor in excess of the permitted statutory amount in your state, it will be necessary either by the terms of your living trust, your last will or by an application to court to appoint an adult called a "custodian", "trustee" or "property guardian" to receive the gift on behalf of the minor. Once received, this person will manage the property on behalf of the child until the child reaches an age set out by you in your living trust or will, or an age prescribed by law.

There are three basic methods for leaving property to minor children or young beneficiaries under your living trust; they are as follows:

(i)   Custodianship

The Uniform Transfers to Minors Act provides a mechanism by which gifts can be made to a minor without requiring the formal appointment of a guardian. Under the act, you can name a person in your living trust to act as "custodian" of a gift made to a young beneficiary. That custodian will receive and manage the property on behalf of the beneficiary until he or she reaches a particular age, at which time the custodianship will end, and the custodian will transfer the property to the beneficiary. While this 'age of termination' varies from state to state, it is usually between 18 to 25 years. This act has been adopted by every state in the U.S. other than South Carolina and Vermont.

Make Your Living Trust Online

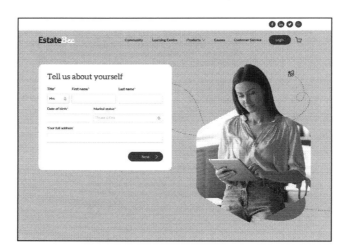

If you wish to create a children's pot trust, we recommend using EstateBee's online estate planning software as it contains a number of flexible options that cannot reasonably be catered for in 'fill-in-the-blank' type documents. For more information visit **www.estate-bee. com/product/online-living-trust/**

(ii) A Child's Trust

It is also possible to create a 'child's sub-trust' under the terms of your living trust for the benefit of a child or a young adult. Your trust agreement will provide for the creation of a sub-trust and the transfer of some or all the trust assets to that sub-trust upon your death. Once transferred to the sub-trust, the property is ring-fenced and held separately from the property left to any other person under the main living trust. A person will be named as trustee of this sub-trust in the living trust agreement and he will be responsible for the management of the trust property on behalf of the beneficiary until that beneficiary becomes entitled to receive the property in his or her own right. Often, this trustee will be the successor trustee. As the sub-trust property is ring-fenced within the living trust, it is quite common to see more than one child trust created under a living trust, especially where the grantor wishes to benefit a number of young beneficiaries.

(iii) A Family Pot Trust

A family pot trust (or children's pot trust as it is sometimes referred to) is slightly different to a child's sub-trust in that it is established for the benefit of two or more children rather than a single child. A family pot trust is managed by the successor trustee who will have discretion in terms of how the proceeds are distributed between each of the children. If one child needs more funds than the other, the successor trustee is at liberty to apply the trust funds as he sees fit.

We discuss each of these three forms of property management in more detail in the ensuing pages.

Gifts to Charities

If you wish to leave a gift to a charity under your living trust, you should ensure that you provide clear details of the charity to be benefited. In this respect, it is useful to identity the charity by reference to its correct legal name (as it may differ from the 'trading name' commonly used by the charity) as well as its charity registration or tax identification number. You should be aware that several states impose limitations on leaving large portions of your estate (including your trust estate) to charity following your death. Therefore, it is advisable to consult a lawyer if you wish to leave a large part (especially 50% or more) of your entire estate (including your trust estate) to one or more charitable institutions or not-for-profit organizations.

Failed Gifts

A gift under your will can fail if the item to be gifted is disposed of or destroyed prior to your death. Where the gift fails, the intended beneficiary will not ordinarily be entitled to receive a substitute gift unless you have specified otherwise in your living trust. Similarly, a gift made to a person that predeceases you will also usually fail. Where it does, the gift becomes part of the residuary trust estate unless you have named an alternate beneficiary who is entitled to receive that gift if the first name beneficiary is unable or unwilling to receive it.

Disinheritance

While the laws vary from state to state, the only people that generally have a right to inherit from your estate are your spouse, children, and grandchildren. However, it is possible to disinherit your children intentionally or unintentionally and, to a lesser extent, your spouse in most states. You can intentionally disinherit your children by intentionally failing to name them in your will or living trust, or by making a nominal gift to them. You can also unintentionally disinherit children by accidentally failing to mention them in your will or living trust. Spouses are a little harder to disinherit because of their entitlement to an elective share of your estate but you can construct your will and living trust so that they only receive the minimum entitlement that the law affords them. Of course, if you try to disinherit family members, they may challenge the terms of your will or living trust in court (although we have discussed the difficulty in doing so in earlier chapters). The success of any such claims would ultimately depend on the laws of your state, the claimant in question and the circumstances surrounding the disinheritance. If you wish to disinherit a family member, speak to an attorney.

Disinheriting Your Spouse

As already mentioned, in most states you cannot simply disinherit your spouse. If you live in a community property state, then your spouse is generally entitled to half of your community property. On the other hand, if you live in a common law state, the law allows spouses to legally claim up to half of your estate regardless of the terms of your will and living trust. It is, therefore, quite difficult to disinherit a spouse from his or her full legal entitlement – although you can leave them with less than your entire estate.

Disinheriting Your Child

By contrast to spouses, and much unlike the laws in other common law countries, it is possible to completely disinherit children in virtually every state in the U.S. In order to disinherit a child, your will and living trust must either (i) expressly state that you intend to disinherit your child or (ii) make only a nominal gift to the child (such as a gift of $10, for example). If you fail to adopt either of these two approaches and simply fail to mention your child in your will or your living trust, then you will run the risk of a court making a determination that there was an accidental disinheritance. In which case, the court could order a re-distribution of your estate (including your trust estate) to include a share for the omitted child.

Moreover, in some states, the disinheritance laws apply not only to children but also to grandchildren. Where the laws do apply, grandchildren can challenge the will of a deceased grandparent who failed to provide for them or for their dead parent. As such, it is important to ensure that grandchildren are expressly disinherited in the same way as children if it is in fact your intention to disinherit both sets of descendants.

In certain circumstances, children are entitled to claim a share of a deceased parent's property, regardless of the terms of their parent's will or living trust. For example, if you live in the state of Florida and are the head of your family for tax purposes, you will be prohibited from leaving your home under your will to anyone other than your spouse or children.

If you have a child born after your will or living trust is made, then it will be necessary for you to make a new will or amend your living trust in order to disinherit that child even where your existing will or living trust already states that you wish to disinherit all of your children. This is because it will be presumed that you only intended to disinherit your children who were alive at the time you made your will and living trust and not those born afterwards.

If you plan on disinheriting a child, be sure to check the applicable laws in your state and speak to your attorney.

Children's Inheritances & Property Guardians

Children under the age of majority lack sufficient legal capacity to receive and manage inherited property. While this lack of capacity is often not an issue for most minors, it can become a problem when they inherit significant or valuable assets. In such cases, it becomes necessary to appoint an adult called a "custodian", "trustee", "conservator" or "property guardian" to receive and manage the property on their behalf.

A property guardian will have full responsibility for the management of property left to a child under his care. He will be required to manage that property in the best interests of the child and, where appropriate, apply it towards the child's normal living expenses, as well as his or her health and educational needs.

While a property guardian can be appointed under the terms of a will, the scope of his management authority extends beyond the management of property left to a child under that will. In fact, it extends to include any property later received by that child in circumstances where no arrangements (whether under the terms of your living trust or otherwise) have been made for the management of that property on his or her behalf. By way of illustration, if the child receives an inheritance from a long lost relative, his or her property guardian will be authorized to manage that property on behalf of the child if the relative has not provided for a specific means of managing it.

Failing to Designate a Property Guardian

If you fail to nominate a property guardian under your will, whether for your children or another minor beneficiary, the court will do so for you by appointing a person of its choosing to act as the child's property guardian. A court will often appoint the surviving parent, but this is not always the case. A third party or court appointed guardian can be appointed to manage the property on behalf of the minor and, in such cases, that property guardian will have complete control over the minor's inheritance. It follows that if you want to retain control over the appointment, it is important that you nominate a property guardian in your will (as well as in your living trusts) or in another legal document.

Options for Property Management

Fortunately, it is relatively easy and straightforward to avoid the uncertainties and hassles of a court-appointed guardianship. You can choose someone now to manage any property that your minor or young adult children may someday inherit from you. While there are many ways that you can structure this arrangement, including the appointment of property guardians, three of the simplest and most common methods are discussed below.

Uniform Transfer to Minors' Act

Minors in most states do not have the legal capacity to enter legal contracts and are therefore not able to own and manage stocks, bonds, funds, life insurances and other annuities. As a result, it is important to recognize that you cannot simply transfer any of these items directly to minor children under your living trust.

One of the most common methods of getting around this problem is to create a trust. On your death, and provided the relevant terms are included in your will or living trust agreement, a trust will be automatically created for the benefit of a named child beneficiary. Simultaneously with the creation of that trust, the assets left to that child under your will or living trust agreement will be transferred into the trust, to be held and managed by a trustee for the benefit of the child. During the term of that trust, the trustee will usually have discretion to provide for the child's needs and welfare from the trust fund (resulting in a depletion of the balance of the trust fund over time).

Once the child reaches the age of legal majority in his state or a specific age set out in the living trust or will (known as the "age of termination"), the trust will automatically terminate and the balance of the trust property will be transferred to the child free from the provisions of the trust.

Trusts were historically perceived as complicated and expensive to set up. Fortunately, the Uniform Gift to Minors Act ("**UMGA**") sought to end this perception by creating a quite simple way for assets to be transferred to minors without the need for lawyers, complicated trusts, and the associated legal costs. It operated by allowing a testator or grantor to simply gift property to a custodian (like a trustee) named in his will or living trust to be held by that custodian until the child was of sufficient age to receive the inheritance. In much the same way as a trust set out what a trustee could and couldn't do, and what he should do, the UGMA did much the same for custodians thereby creating a simple framework for creating trusts or 'custodianships'.

The UGMA was repealed in large part by the Uniform Transfer to Minors Act ("**UTMA**"). The UTMA, while similar in its approach to the UGMA, is widely considered to be more flexible. This is because it also applies to property received by inheritance rather than only to property received by means of a gift from a living person; and because it allowed minors to receive additional types of property such as real estate, patents and royalties. The UTMA has been adopted in all states except for Vermont and South Carolina.

In order to set up a custodianship, all you need to do is identify the trust property that you wish to gift, the name of the child you wish to make the gift to and the name of person who will act as the child's custodian. Then simply gift the property to the custodian to hold on behalf of the child until he or she is old enough to receive the gift. A typical clause of this type would be written something like this: -

"I give $25,000 to James Jones, as custodian for Sarah Parker under the California Uniform Transfers to Minors Act."

Age of Termination

As mentioned, the age of termination is the statutory age at which a minor becomes legally entitled to call for the assets held by a custodian under the UTMA to be transferred to him and to have the custodial trust terminated. The table below shows the age which minors must reach in each state before a custodial trust created in that state can terminate. Where a range of ages is provided, the grantor or testator will be entitled to choose an age from that range at which the custodial trust will terminate.

Age Limits for Property Management in UTMA States			
State	Age at Which Minor Gets Property	State	Age at Which Minor Gets Property
Alabama	21	Missouri	21
Alaska	18 to 25	Montana	21
Arizona	21	Nebraska	21
Arkansas	18 to 21	Nevada	18 to 25
California	18 to 25	New Hampshire	21
Colorado	21	New Jersey	18 to 21
Connecticut	21	New Mexico	21
Delaware	21	New York	21
District of Columbia	18 to 21	North Carolina	18 to 21
Florida	21	North Dakota	21
Georgia	21	Ohio	18 to 21
Hawaii	21	Oklahoma	18 to 21
Idaho	21	Oregon	21 to 25
Illinois	21	Pennsylvania	21 to 25
Indiana	21	Rhode Island	21
Iowa	21	South Dakota	18
Kansas	21	Tennessee	21 to 25
Kentucky	18	Texas	21
Maine	18 to 21	Utah	21

Maryland	21	Virginia	18 to 21
Massachusetts	21	Washington	21
Michigan	18 to 21	West Virginia	21
Minnesota	21	Wisconsin	21
Mississippi	21	Wyoming	21

Child Sub-Trusts

A child's sub-trust is valid in all U.S. states and can be created under the terms of a living trust agreement. To create a child's sub-trust under your living trust, you will need to provide for the creation of that trust in your living trust using certain required legal language. You will also need to name the person who will act as trustee of that trust (which is usually the successor trustee), the child or young beneficiary who will be entitled to receive the trust assets held in that trust and the age at which he will be entitled to do so – which can be any age above the age of majority (although 18 – 25 years is the norm). If the child is already over this age at the time of your death, and has reached the age of majority in his state, the sub-trust will never actually come into existence and the sub-trust property will instead be transferred directly to the child upon your death.

On the other hand, if the proposed child beneficiary is under the sub-trust's age of termination at the time of your death, the sub-trust will be created and the relevant property will be deemed to have been transferred into the sub-trust fund. Thereafter, those trust assets will be managed by the successor trustee in accordance with provisions set out in your living trust agreement. The successor trustee will manage those assets until the child beneficiary has reached the age specified in the living trust agreement. At that time, the remainder of the sub-trust assets will be transferred to him and the trust will be terminated.

During the sub-trust, the successor trustee will have broad discretion over the management and distribution of the sub-trust assets. If the successor trustee deems it appropriate, monies can usually be released to the child from time to time to cover matters ranging from education to medical treatment to general maintenance.

Children's and Family Pot Trusts

A pot trust is also a good tool to use with younger children as it allows you to place monies into another sub-trust to benefit two or more children. These types of trust are somewhat unique in that the trust assets can be made available to whichever child needs them the most rather than being divided equally for the benefit of each child beneficiary. In this regard, the successor trustee will have discretion to apportion the family pot trust fund between the child beneficiaries as he sees fit. For example, if one of your child beneficiaries wishes to go to college, your successor trustee can take a portion of the money from the pot trust to send that child to college. Similarly, should one of the beneficiaries require an expensive medical treatment, monies can be released from the pot trust to cover the costs of the treatment.

A pot trust will terminate when the youngest child reaches a specific age set out in the living trust agreement - which is usually an age between 18 and 25 years. At that time, the proceeds of the pot trust will be divided between the beneficiaries equally. One of the principal drawbacks to using a pot trust is, however, that older children cannot receive their final share of the trust property until the youngest child reaches the designated age of termination. As such, in certain cases, some of the beneficiaries could be well into adulthood by the time they receive their share of the inheritance.

CHAPTER 8

Estate Taxes

Important Note

For tax purposes, living trusts are treated as being tax transparent. In other words, when it comes to assessing a person to tax, the IRS will look through the existence of a living trust and treat the trust property as if it still belongs to the grantor.

Estate Taxes

When accountants, lawyers and others who deal with these matters refer to 'estate tax' they are usually referring to federal tax, not state tax. This distinction is made for three main reasons: (i) many states do not impose an inheritance or death tax; (ii) federal tax is likely to devour more of an estate than state tax will; and (iii) reducing the federal estate tax will often result in a reduction of state taxes as well.

Federal Estate and Gift Tax

The U.S. tax system generally taxes transfers of wealth. This means the federal government usually charges a tax when money or other assets are transferred from one person to another. Keeping this general rule in mind helps to understand estate and gift taxes.

Gift tax, unlike most income taxes, is assessed on the giver, and not the receiver. As such, if you make a gift of cash or an asset to someone, you will be assessed to a gift tax unless you fall within the scope of the exceptions set out under the headings below. When gift tax is payable, you will need to record details of the gift on IRS form 709. Like many other tax forms, the gift tax form is generally due April 15th in the year following the year in which you made the gift.

Similarly, when you die, another transfer of assets takes place from you to someone else. Like the gift tax, the estate tax is imposed on the giver, which in that case will be your estate. A federal estate tax return is reported on IRS form 706 and is due to be filed with the IRS within nine months of the date of your death unless extended.

Everyone's "Coupon"

The gift and estate tax have to be considered together, because they are intertwined in that both are taken into account when calculating the maximum amount that you can give away or, if you die, your estate can transfer without incurring a charge to tax. Simply speaking, the maximum amount you can transfer without incurring gift or estate tax is like a "coupon". When the value of your gifts and estate are calculated, you can apply this "coupon" to minimize or avoid the tax. You will only have to pay gift or estate tax if your gifts and/or transfers exceed this "coupon" amount.

For example, in 2021 the "coupon" for gifts and estates is $11.7 million. That means that you can transfer up to $11.7 million in gifts during your lifetime and there will not be any gift tax due. If the gift is made to someone other than your spouse, it will not matter who received the gift just that the total value of gifts did not exceed the "coupon". However, if you exceed the value of the "coupon", you will owe tax on the excess gift(s). A chart detailing the rate of gift and estate tax can be found under the section below entitled "How to Determine the Estate Tax".

For example, if you give $5 million of taxable gifts to each of your three children over your lifetime, you will have made $5 million in taxable gifts. You can use your "coupon" to avoid tax on the first $11.7 million but you will owe tax on the other $3.3 million.

How does this relate to estate taxes? Well, for most years, you also have a "coupon" for estate taxes. However, as the government views every dollar you gave away during your lifetime as a dollar less that can be taxed in your estate when you die, this "coupon" will be reduced by the amount of the gift tax "coupon" that you have used during your lifetime! So, while there is also a "coupon" for estate tax, it is linked to the gift tax "coupon"; and more specifically to the amount of that gift tax "coupon" that you have already used.

Example of Coupon Calculation

Anna died in 2021, when the lifetime gifting exemption was $11.7 million. During her lifetime, she gave James and John a total of $10 million in gifts. The amount of those gifts is deducted from her estate tax exemption of $11.7 million to determine her remaining estate tax exception. In this case, it would be $1.7 million ($11.7 million minus the $10 million gift tax exemption used).

How to Determine the Estate Tax?

The first question to ask when trying to determine the amount of federal estate tax which might be due by your estate is "What is the fair market value of everything you own, control, or have an interest in at the date of your death?" In answering this question, you will need to include all assets you own such as cash, investments, real estate, and personal property such as cars, boats, art, and the like. Estate tax is also levied on the life insurance policies in your name where you have a right of ownership in the policy.

The total value of all these items is called your "gross estate". Your taxable estate is your gross estate less certain deductions. These deductions may include mortgages on your assets, debts you owe, estate administration expenses, property that passes automatically to your surviving spouse on your death, and bequests to qualified charities (more on the deductions for spouses and charities below). The value of your gross estate minus these deductions is referred to as your "taxable estate".

Once you have calculated your taxable estate, estate tax may be owed if the value of the taxable estate exceeds the unused portion of your estate tax "coupon."

Just as the value of the "coupon" changes depending on the year in which you make a gift or die, the percentage of the tax assessment also changes.

Year of Gift/Death	Maximum Gift Tax	Maximum Estate Tax
2009	45%	45%
2010	35%	N/A
2011 & 2012	35%	35%
2013 - 2021	40%	40%

State Taxes

Not every state imposes a separate state tax on estates or inheritances. Florida, for instance, imposes no state death tax. Where there is such a tax, it is likely to be one (or a combination) of three types of tax: (1) death tax, (2) inheritance tax, or (3) pick-up tax.

State Death Taxes

Generally, when people use the phrase "death tax", they are referring to state taxes levied by the state on a deceased person's estate upon death. The amount of state tax due, if any, is determined on a state-by-state basis according to that state's tax laws and is often calculated in a manner similar to federal estate tax.

State Inheritance Taxes

In states with inheritance tax laws, inheritance tax is usually paid by the person who receives assets either under a will or on intestacy. In some states, the tax is levied on the estate itself so that the tax must be paid by the estate before calculating what can be distributed to beneficiaries. One tax rate may apply to all assets in the estate, or the rate may vary depending upon who receives what property. Generally, the closer the person receiving a gift from the deceased is to the deceased (in terms of blood line), the lower the tax rate on the transfer of property to that person. Thus, depending on what class the beneficiary falls into, he or she will be taxed at a specific rate.

States with Inheritance Taxes or State Estate Taxes			
State	Tax Collected	State	Tax Collected
Connecticut	Estate Tax	Nebraska	Inheritance Tax
Delaware	Estate Tax, expires on July 1, 2013	New Jersey	Estate Tax and Inheritance Tax
District of Columbia	Estate Tax	New York	Estate Tax
Hawaii	Estate Tax	North Carolina	Estate Tax
Illinois	Estate Tax	Oregon	Estate Tax
Iowa	Inheritance Tax	Pennsylvania	Inheritance Tax
Kentucky	Inheritance Tax	Rhode Island	Estate Tax
Maine	Estate Tax	Tennessee	Estate Tax
Maryland	Estate Tax & Inheritance Tax	Vermont	Estate Tax
Massachusetts	Estate Tax	Washington	Estate Tax
Minnesota	Estate Tax		

State "Pick-Up" Taxes

Some states base all or a portion of their state death tax on the amount of estate tax credit allowed against payments of state death taxes. Prior to 2005, federal estate taxes could be reduced by a credit for state death taxes paid on an estate. The result was that the federal estate tax was a "maximum" tax that was paid partly to the state and partly to the federal government. Many states therefore would "pick-up" their tax revenue by pegging their state death taxes at the amount of the federal credit that you could claim for state death taxes. After 2001, the federal government gradually eliminated the credit for state death taxes. However, some states chose to continue to charge a pick-up tax based on what the federal credit was in 2001, even though the federal credit is no longer available.

For all three of the types of tax a state might assess, some states will have a "coupon" equal to the federal tax "coupon", meaning that if there is no federal estate tax there is no state estate tax. However, many states have chosen not to increase their "coupons" at the same rate that the federal law does, so the state "coupon" may be smaller, resulting in state estate tax being payable even where federal estate tax is not payable.

Marital Deduction

Remember the gift and estate tax "coupon" for federal taxes? Historically, it was unique to each individual/estate and could not be used by anyone else. That meant that you had a "coupon", and your spouse had a "coupon", and they were non-transferable.

The "coupons" are not used up by gifts made or estates transferred to a spouse who is a U.S. citizen. Instead, federal gift/estate tax applies an unlimited deduction to those transfers. In other words, you can gift or transfer an unlimited amount of property to your U.S. citizen spouse and there is no gift or estate tax on that transfer.

That is the good news. The bad news is that the marital deduction is, in some ways, just a waiting game whereby the government allows you to transfer your property tax free to your spouse with the view that it will later be taxed when your spouse dies or gives it away. As your spouse could not use your gift/ estate tax "coupon" prior to the introduction of the Tax Relief, Unemployment Insurance Reauthorization, and Job Creation Act of 2010, in December 2010, that meant that your spouse had more to transfer to her beneficiaries and heirs but without the benefit of an increased the "coupon". However, in December 2010, President Obama signed this legislation into law which entitled a person to use any unused element of his or her deceased spouse's coupon. However, that right would be lost if the surviving spouse remarried and then her new spouse predeceased her.

Consider this example: Your last will & testament provides for your spouse to inherit everything you own when you die. At your death, your net taxable estate is $12 million, and your spouse has an estate worth $12 million. Since your spouse was the recipient of your estate, the unlimited marital deduction applies and there is no estate tax due because of your death regardless of the applicable "coupon". If your spouse dies in 2021, under current law your spouse's maximum "coupon" will be $23.4 million – being $11.7 million of his or her own plus $11.7 million of yours – assuming neither of you previously used any element of your coupon. Of course, to the extent that either of you used your coupon, this amount will be deducted from the $23.4 million coupon. Ultimately, your spouse's estate will be subject to tax on the excess of $600,000 ($24 million minus $23.4 million). At a tax rate of 40%, that translates to a tax of $240,000.

Important Note

A surviving spouse may lose the right to use his or her deceased spouse's coupon if he or she remarries.

Non-Citizen Spouses

The unlimited marital deduction is available only when you give or leave your assets to a spouse who is a U.S. citizen at the time the transfer is made. Some types of credit shelter trust planning mechanisms are also only effective if your spouse is a U.S. citizen. If your spouse is not a citizen, your estate plan must include more sophisticated trust planning designed to keep the assets in the United States managed by a U.S. trustee so that the trust can qualify for the marital deduction that is otherwise only available to U.S. citizen spouses. This is called a Qualified Domestic Trust, or QDOT. For more information, speak to your attorney.

Charitable Deductions

You probably already know that you get an income tax deduction when you donate to a charity during your lifetime. You can also save on estate taxes by giving to charity. Any bequest you make from your estate to a qualified charity is exempt from federal estate tax. You can also combine estate tax planning and income tax planning by setting up a trust with a charity as one of the beneficiaries.

Charitable Remainder Trust

The most common charitable trust is a charitable remainder trust, or CRT. With this type of trust, you donate an asset or assets to the trust during your lifetime. You can continue to get some income from the trust assets, but the charity gets the remainder of what is in the trust when you die or when the term of the trust otherwise ends. Because you have donated to the trust, you will be allowed to take an income tax deduction equal to the estimated value of the charity's remainder. You have also removed the asset in the trust from your estate, so it will not be subject to estate taxes when you die. Yet you still can enjoy a regular payout from the trust assets. The amount of income you get from the trust may be either a fixed percentage of the assets you donated to the trust or a percentage of the trust's value each year. Of course, if you choose to peg your payment on the value of the trust, your payment will fluctuate as the value of the assets in the trust fluctuates.

Some CRTs are especially attractive if you have assets that have appreciated in value. By placing the asset into the trust, you may be able to minimize the capital gains taxes you would otherwise have had to pay when you sold the asset.

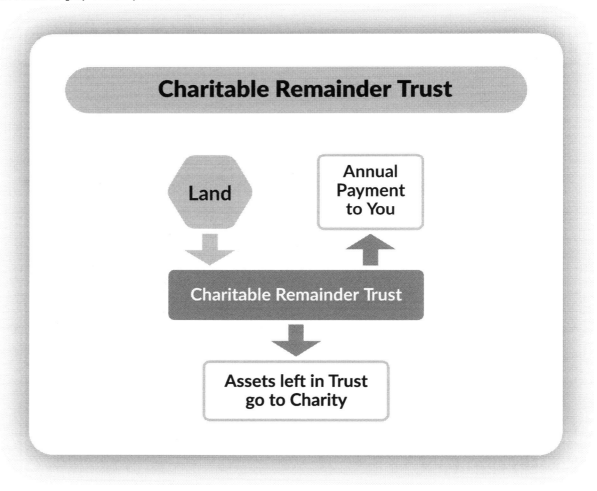

Let us look at how a CRT would work in an example: Anna and David own vacant land that they purchased many years ago. The value of the land has gone up considerably, so they would have to pay significant capital gains tax if they sold it. Yet, the land is not producing any income for them in their retirement. Rather than sell the land, pay the capital gains tax, and then invest the after-tax proceeds to produce income, they decide to create a CRT and donate the land to the trust. Once the land has been transferred to the trust, the trust is free to sell the land without having to pay any capital gains tax on the sale. The CRT can then use the proceeds of sale to provide an income to Anna and David for as long as any one of them is alive. After they both die, the remainder of the trust assets can be given to a charity of their choosing.

Having established the CRT and transferred the land to it, Anna and David take an immediate income tax deduction for the estimated value of the amount that the trust will give to their chosen charity. In addition, they will receive income annually from the trust. They may have to pay some tax on the income they receive from the trust, but often it is not as much as they would have had to pay upfront if they had just sold the land. Furthermore, the value of the land is no longer in their estates, so there will not be any estate tax assessed on that value – which is a further cost saving to their estate.

Charitable Lead Trust

Another type of charitable trust is a charitable lead trust ("CLT"). With a CLT, you transfer property to a trust that then pays an annual income ("the lead") to a charity. When the trust terminates after a specified number of years, the remaining assets left in the trust go to a person or persons you name, such as your children. Generally, you won't get an income tax deduction for giving any property to a CLT, but you won't pay any gift tax and you have removed some of the value of the asset from your estate. A CLT can be a good choice for an asset that is expected to appreciate in the future, so that the appreciated value will not be in your estate.

Another example: Assume that Anna and David in the example above have land that they expect to be worth much more in the coming years as the area around the land is developed. They decide to establish a charitable lead trust that in five years will begin to pay a percentage of the trust assets to their favorite charity. When the trust is terminated in fifteen years, the assets remaining in the trust will go to their grandchildren. There may be a taxable gift to the grandchildren depending on the estimated value of the gift that passes to them, but that estimated value will be based on the value of the land now, and will not include the high appreciation expected in the near future. Anna and David have removed the value of the asset from their estate, provided for their favorite charity, and assured that the land as it appreciates will benefit their grandchildren in the future.

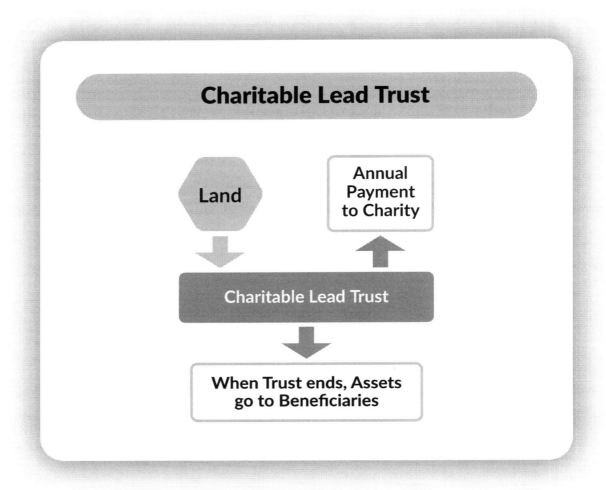

For more information on CLTs, speak to your attorney or tax advisor.

Other Ways to Reduce Estate Taxes

Federal estate tax can be reduced through a variety of other legitimate estate planning techniques. Since the "coupon" has increased to $11.7 million per person, those with large estates over this amount could benefit from considering some of the methods listed below to reduce potential estate tax liability. The advantages and disadvantages of these techniques vary greatly depending on the individual circumstances of the persons using them. That is why having an experienced attorney or tax advisor can be beneficial as you consider how these techniques fit your situation.

Lifetime Gifts

Under federal tax law, some gifts incur no gift tax, do not require filing of a gift tax return, and do not even use up any of your "coupon". This amount is pegged to inflation so it will vary each year. For example, in 2021 you may make an annual tax-exempt gift to any one person provided the total amount of gifts to that person during the calendar year does not exceed $15,000. This exemption applies to each person making a gift which means that if both you and your spouse utilize this estate planning tool, you could collectively reduce your estate by giving away $30,000 a year to any number of beneficiaries, free of any federal gift tax. The annual exemption amount changes based on inflation, but over a period of several years the amount of money that you and your spouse (or partner) could transfer to your intended beneficiaries under this method could be quite substantial.

You can also make tax-free gifts by paying someone's medical expenses or tuition bills if you pay the bill directly to the medical or educational institution. Gifts of this type are not subject to the annual exemption limits and can be in any amount.

Making lifetime gifts as described above removes the gifted assets from your estate, potentially reducing the amount your estate would otherwise have to pay in federal estate tax. However, during most years, lifetime gifts may be less advantageous than inheritances when we consider the effect of capital gains taxes. Capital gain is the amount you get when you sell the asset minus your basis. Broadly speaking, basis is the amount you have invested in the asset. So, if you sell an asset for $100 where your basis was $10, you will have a capital gain of $90 that is subject to capital gains tax. When you make a gift during your lifetime, the recipient of the gift has the same basis in the gifted asset as you have. As a result, the $100 asset will have the same $90 capital gain when the recipient sells it as you would have incurred if you had sold it. The transfer of the initial $10 basis to the recipient in this manner is referred to as a "carry-over basis".

However, in if you leave the asset as an inheritance rather than a lifetime gift, your recipient now gets a "stepped up basis" to the value of the asset on the date that you died. In the case of our $100 asset, if the value were $100 when you died, the recipient would now have a basis of $100 (rather than a carry-over basis of $10). If the recipient sells the asset for $100, there will be no capital gains subject to tax. Since capital gains taxes are currently around 15%, gifting the asset would have cost the recipient $13.50 in capital gains tax ($90 x .15) while inheriting the asset would not have incurred any tax. This difference in basis is why it is important to consult a tax advisor before making significant lifetime gifts as part of your estate planning.

Let us consider an example. Assume Adam dies in 2021 leaving all his property to his 3 children. Also assume Adam's entire estate consists of nine apartment houses each worth $1 million dollars. Finally, let us assume that Adam's original basis in each apartment house was $200,000 or a total of $1.8 million in original basis for the total estate. With the basis step up at his death, when Adam's assets are sold by his estate or later by any of his children, those assets will have a total basis of $9 million, which is the value of the properties as of the date of Adam's death. If Adam's estate sells all the apartment houses for $1 million each before distributing the proceeds to Adam's children, those sales would result in no capital gains tax.

If Adam's estate does not sell all the apartment houses but instead transfers them directly to his 3 children, each child would receive 3 apartment houses. While none of his children would have to pay capital gains tax when the inheritance is received, each child would have a basis equal to one-third of the $9 million new basis, or $1 million per apartment house. When a child sells an apartment house, he or she must pay capital gains tax on the difference between the total sales price and the new basis of $1 million.

Now assume that Adam left his estate to his wife Alexandra rather than his children. The capital gains result is the same. Alexandra's new basis in the properties is $9 million, or the value of the properties as of the date of Adam's death.

Based on these examples, you can see the benefit of getting tax advice.

Note: This example assumes that each apartment house has the same original basis. If the original basis is different for each asset, the new basis will also be different for each asset, as the new basis is the proportional share of stepped up basis plus the original basis.

Irrevocable Life Insurance Trusts

An irrevocable life insurance trust creates a trust that is used exclusively to own life insurance. The trust purchases life insurance on your life, and you make gifts to the trust to pay the premiums. The trust may not be revoked and once you place funds into the trust, they cannot be taken back. Upon your death, the life insurance payout to your trust is distributed according to the terms of the trust. Because you do not control the life insurance, it is not considered part of your taxable estate and thus no federal estate taxes are due when the payout is made.

Family Limited Partnerships

A family limited partnership helps families transfer ownership of their closely held businesses to the next generation of business managers. A family limited partnership, or FLP, is created to hold and manage assets. You may transfer those assets to the FLP in exchange for your interest in the partnership. You then gift some of your partnership interest to your children, perhaps over several years.

FLPs can save estate taxes in two ways. First, they can remove from your estate now assets that are likely to appreciate in value. Even though the asset is removed from the estate, you may retain control over the partnership and therefore have continued control over how the asset is managed. Second, the percentage gift you make to your children in an FLP may be valued at less than the same percentage of the value of the underlying assets in the partnership.

For example, assume you establish a partnership with three pieces of real estate each valued at $500,000. The value of the assets in the partnership total $1,500,000. Then you gift a ten percent interest in the partnership to your son. While ten percent of the value of the partnership assets is $150,000 ($1,500,000 x .10), the value of a ten percent interest in the partnership may be appreciably less than $150,000. This is because as a ten percent owner your son does not have control over the assets and there is not likely to be someone willing to pay him $150,000 for the chance to be a minority partner that lacks control. This has the effect of reducing the fair market value of the 10% interest below that of an equivalent percentage value of the underlying properties. In fact, the real value of the ten percent partnership interest depends on many factors, which is why you must be prepared to get a qualified appraisal on the gift when you use an FLP in your planning. For more information, speak to your attorney or tax advisor.

Special Use Real Estate Valuation

Generally, real estate you transfer by way of a gift or on your death is valued based on the assumption that the real estate will be sold for its "highest and best use" value. For example, farmland may be worth much more if it was sold for residential development than as agricultural land. However, you or your estate may be able to claim that the real estate should be valued based on its "actual use" value rather than the "highest and best use" value. This can result in significant tax savings, especially if your family intends to continue using the land as farmland rather than selling it to a developer. Special use valuation is complicated and generally requires the assistance of an experienced attorney and valuation agent.

Conclusion

Estate taxes and estate tax planning are a complicated area of the law. If you have an estate greater than a million dollars or have other special circumstances, we recommend that you seek professional advice before employing any of the tax reduction strategies referred to in this chapter.

CHAPTER 9

Transferring Assets to Your Living Trust

Introduction

You will recall that there are two primary reasons for establishing a revocable living trust. The first is to provide for the management of your trust property during any period in which you are incapacitated and unable to manage it yourself. The second is to avoid the costs and delays that are usually associated with the probate process. Both are perfectly legitimate and solid reasons for setting up a living trust. However, if you set up a living trust and fail to properly transfer your assets to that trust, or 'fund the trust' as the term is called, your efforts will have been in vain. This is because in the absence of complying with the legal formalities necessary to transfer your assets to your living trust, title and ownership of those assets will remain with you personally. Assets held in your own name will end up going through the probate process following your death; or the intestate administration process if you die without having a valid last will and testament. It is therefore important to take the time to ensure that the title to the assets you 'transfer' to your living trust is properly vested in the trust's name.

What Assets Should Be Put in Your Living Trust?

Given that the costs of probating your estate will most likely be linked to the value of your estate, it makes sense to at least consider transferring some of your most valuable assets to your living trust. However, the decision as to what you transfer to your living trust is entirely up to you. There are no set rules here.

You are free to include assets such as your home and other real estate, bank and saving accounts, investments, business interests, antiques, jewelry, personal belongings, royalties, patents, copyrights, stocks, bonds and other securities, money market accounts and so on.

In deciding what assets you would like to transfer to your living trust, bear in mind that you will be acting as both grantor and trustee of your living trust. As such, you will have the right to call for the return of any assets you transfer to the trust at any time – provided of course the living trust is revocable. As such, if having transferred assets to your trust, you subsequently get uncomfortable (for whatever reason) with the whole situation, you can simply use your powers as grantor and trustee to take back the assets.

While you are free to transfer whatever assets you wish to your trust, the reality is that you do not need to put everything into your trust to save money on probate. As you will have already seen from Chapter 2, not all assets go through probate. As such, while you could in theory transfer some of those assets to your living trust, there is generally no need to do so. This is particularly so in the case of assets that can pass to designated beneficiaries automatically on your death.

Take an insurance policy, for example. If you transfer the benefit of that policy to your living trust, then your living trust will receive the lump sum payment from the insurance company when you die. If you wish to make a gift of those funds to a specific person, you can do so under your living trust. However, the beneficiary will have to wait until your successor trustee is able to distribute the trust assets to the beneficiaries named in the living trust agreement. This may not happen until all the trust's expenses have been paid and its creditors paid. As such, in these circumstances, it would perhaps have been easier to simply designate the intended beneficiary as a beneficiary under the insurance policy. In that way, the funds would have been paid directly to him.

In the list below, we have set out details of some of the items which are commonly not transferred to living trusts: -

(i) Automobiles (where they are exempt from probate).

(ii) Retirement accounts (particularly IRAs, 401(k)s and profit-sharing plans).

(iii) Pay-on-death accounts.

(iv) Property which you buy and sell frequently.

(v) Life Insurance. **

Important Note

** When you take out a life insurance policy, you typically designate beneficiaries of that policy within the insurance documentation. By doing so, the beneficiaries become entitled to receive the proceeds of the insurance policy on your death - free from the need to have those proceeds go through probate. However, if you wish to gift those proceeds to a young beneficiary and have an adult manage those proceeds on behalf of the beneficiary, you could designate your living trust as the beneficiary of the insurance proceeds under your insurance documentation. Then, in the trust agreement, you can make an equivalent cash gift to the young beneficiary and create a child's sub-trust for the purpose of providing for the management of those funds on the beneficiary's behalf.

Transferring Title in Assets to a Living Trust

Historically, there has been considerable debate amongst legal academics as to whether property transferred to a living trust needed to be re-titled in the name of the trust. The consensus was that where the same person acted as both grantor and trustee of a trust there was no need to formally transfer title. The mere inclusion of a reference to the transferred asset on the schedule of assets attached to the living trust agreement was generally regarded as being sufficient. However, certain states (such as New York) require the formal transfer of items such as real estate, securities, bank accounts, etc. As such, the best practice approach is to re-title all assets that have any form of title document in the name of the trust. This helps remove a lot of the ambiguity surrounding the issue.

In order to re-title an asset registered in your name to the name of your living trust, all you need to do is sign a document transferring the legal title in that asset from you to the trust. That transfer will, for example, be made between (1) John Smith and (2) John Smith, acting as trustee of the John Smith Family Living Trust dated 1 January 2021. When it comes to signing the transfer agreement, you will sign it in your own name as transferor as well as signing it on behalf of the living trust as transferee. When signing on behalf of the living trust, you will sign it using words such as "John Smith, Trustee".

Employer Identification Numbers

If you act as both grantor and trustee of your living trust, the trust will be considered transparent for tax purposes. As such, you will not need to obtain a separate tax identification number for it. You will simply use your own personal tax number for the trust. However, if you appoint a third party to act as trustee of the trust (as sole trustee) or if the successor trustee steps-in to take control of the trust during any period in which you are incapacitated or following your death, a separate employer tax identification number will need to be obtained.

The process of obtaining a new employer tax identification number for a trust is relatively straight forward. All that your trustee or successor trustee will need to do is complete an Internal Revenue Service Form SS-4 and return it to the IRS. Once processed, the IRS should issue your trust with its very own tax number. Following the issue of that tax number, the trust's tax returns will cease to be made using your tax number and will need to be made by the trust using its own tax number.

It is also worth mentioning that, in addition to looking for a taxpayer identification number, many financial institutions and third parties will require a copy of the trust agreement when dealing with a living trust. As the living trust agreement will invariably contain personal information such as details of the assets held, the proposed beneficiaries, the gifts proposed to be made to them, etc., it is a good idea to avoid producing the entire document. Fortunately, this can be done using an Affidavit of Trust (or Certification of Trust, as it is also called). An Affidavit of Trust is a declaration sworn by you in front of a notary public confirming that you are the trustee of the trust and attaching relevant pages of the trust (but not all of them) to evidence your appointment as trustee and the signature of both grantor and trustee. This affidavit is generally acceptable by most third parties and should help preserve the confidentiality of the trust terms – which is important especially if you live in a small town. A sample affidavit is contained at the back of this book, although it has been drafted to reflect the terms of the living trust agreements accompanying this book. As such, if you wish to use the affidavit with another living trust, you may need to amend its terms as appropriate. Of course, you can also have your lawyer prepare one if you wish.

How to Transfer Specific Property to a Trust

As already stated, the best way to ensure that your assets are transferred to your living trust is by using a formal deed of transfer. It is best not to rely on the presumption that naming an asset in the schedule to your trust agreement is sufficient to transfer title in that asset to your trust. If the IRS or someone else successfully challenges that presumption, the asset will be deemed to be held in your name and will have to go through probate or intestate administration.

Given the vast diversity of the assets that you could potentially transfer to your living trust, it's worthwhile taking a look at how some of the more commonly held assets are usually transferred to a living trust.

Real Estate

To transfer real estate or real property, as it is often called, to your living trust you will need to prepare a deed of transfer. In most cases this can be straightforward. However, there are certain issues that you need to watch out for as there are many different nuances associated with the transfer of title to real estate. As such, we recommend that you engage the services of an attorney qualified in your state to assist with the transfer of any property located in your state.

Types of Deed

When dealing with property transfers, you will usually have two different types of deed that you can use to transfer the property – namely a "warranty deed" and a "quitclaim deed". There is little real difference between the two deeds save that a warranty deed provides a warranty that the seller has a good marketable title to the property being transferred, and a quitclaim deed does not. While you may take the view that, as you are transferring property held in your name to your living trust, it really does not matter too much which deed you use. To a large extent, that is true. However, problems can arise down the line where your successor trustee attempts to sell the property. Potential purchasers may be reluctant to purchase the property from the trust as it will be selling the property without the benefit of having received warranties from the previous seller. In which case, potential purchasers will be concerned that there is a deficiency in the trust's title to the property. In addition, the purchaser's lending institution may refuse to provide finance in connection with the acquisition of a property that has title issues. This can make it exceedingly difficult for the trust to sell the property in question.

If you are transferring real estate to your trust, we recommend that you consult your attorney. Your attorney should also be able to ensure that the title deed transferring the real estate to the trust is properly registered in the relevant land registry.

Mortgage

If your property is mortgaged, you will need to obtain the consent of the lending institution to the transfer of the property before you transfer it to the trust. Most mortgage documents contain clauses which allow lending institutions to call for the full and immediate payment of all sums secured against the property if it is transferred without the lender's prior written consent. You should carefully check the position with the lender before signing a deed of transfer in respect of the property.

Title Insurance

The transfer of your property to your living trust may terminate any existing title insurance policies covering your property. As such, you should check the position with your insurance provider before making the transfer. If it transpires that the transfer will terminate the policy, you should consider having the policy re-instated once the transfer to the trust has been completed. If the property is mortgaged, your lender may insist on the policy being reinstated.

Out-of-State Property

If you have any property located out-of-state, it is recommended that you engage an attorney licensed and practicing in that state to deal with the transfer of that particular property. Most states have slightly different requirements when it comes to transferring real property and dealing with associated matters such as title insurance. As such, an attorney located in the state in which the property is located will generally be best placed to advise on the particular aspects of the transfer, and ensure that all of the required formalities relating to the transfer of the property to the trust are complied with.

Homestead Rights

Each state has specific legislation which protects a principal private residence or family home from creditors if one of the spouses becomes bankrupt. However, recent case law in some states has called into question whether this protection could be lost if the family home is transferred into a living trust. The laws vary from state to state on this point and, in some states, are not firmly settled. It is therefore recommended that you seek the advice of an attorney before transferring your family home to your living trust.

Tax on Transfers

Ordinarily, tax will not be payable on the transfer of property into a living trust. However, this varies from state to state so you should check this with an attorney to confirm the position.

Tangible Personal Property

Tangible personal property is property (other than real property such as land and buildings) that you can touch. This would include items such as your car, boat, antiques, stamp collection, jewelry, household furniture, computer equipment and so on. To transfer personal property to your living trust, it is recommended that you use a deed of assignment like that at Appendix 5. It may not be absolutely required as a matter of law, but from a practical perspective it reduces the likelihood that a third party could argue that the asset was not properly transferred to your trust.

Cars, Boats and Other Vehicles

You can transfer a vehicle to your trust in much the same way as you would transfer it to a third party. However, as the majority of states have specific forms that need to be used when registering the transfer of a vehicle, you will need to check with the relevant department of motor vehicles to determine the precise forms that will need to be used. Be aware that, in some states, a tax can be levied when transferring vehicles from one person to another.

If your boat happens to be registered with the Coast Guard (although very few are), you will need to check with them to determine what their specific transfer requirements are.

Important Note

If you plan on transferring your vehicle or watercraft to your living trust, you should check with your insurer and any person who has provided secured finance in connection with the purchase of the vehicle or watercraft in question. You will most likely require the prior consent of the finance provider before transferring the vehicle/craft, while your insurer will need to change the details of the policy to note the living trust as the new owner or create a new policy for the trust. In several states, vehicles of a certain monitory value do not need to go through probate. As such, you should consider whether there is any real benefit in transferring that vehicle to your living trust. Your local department of motor vehicles should be able to confirm the requisite values for you.

Cash Accounts

Title to checking accounts, savings accounts, money market accounts and certificates of deposit (whether held at a bank or other financial institution) can be transferred into your living trust relatively easily. To make the required transfer, you can either change the name on the account (from say "John Smith" to "John Smith, trustee of John Smith Family Living Trust") or transfer the proceeds of the existing account to a new account in the name of the trust. The financial institution in which the accounts are held can advise you of the methods available to you and which is perhaps the best option for you. However, you should be careful when closing some of these accounts as the closure of accounts of this type can sometimes trigger the payment of small penalties. You will need to check the position carefully in the account documentation or directly with the financial institution. In some cases, if you explain what you are doing (i.e. that you are opening a new account in the name of the living trust into which the proceeds of the closed account will be transferred) the financial institution may waive its fees.

Important Note

When dealing with a financial institution, it may wish to obtain an Affidavit of Trust from you before allowing you to act on behalf of the trust.

United States Savings Bonds

While U.S. savings bonds can be transferred into your living trust, you will need to contact your bank to obtain the appropriate form as well as details of the procedure involved in transferring the bonds to the trust. You will normally need to complete a Treasury Form FS 1455 and send the completed form to the relevant financial institution together with a copy of your Affidavit of Trust and any certificate of title evidencing your holding of the bonds in order to instruct the institution to make the transfer. Once the transfer is completed, the bonds will be re-issued in the name of the living trust.

Broker Accounts

It is possible to transfer a broker account held with a brokerage firm or with a mutual fund company directly to your living trust. You will however need to contact the firm/company to determine whether they can simply change the name on the account or whether they will have to close the existing account and open a new one in the name of the living trust. In dealing with the brokerage firm or mutual fund company, you will most likely need to send it a copy of your Affidavit of Trust and details of the relevant brokerage account.

Publicly Traded Stocks and Bonds

To transfer stocks held by you to your living trust, you will need to contact the company's share registrar (also called a transfer agent) and formally request that the stocks in question be transferred to and re-issued in the name of the living trust. If you are in possession of the stock certificate issued in your name, it should indicate the identity of the share registrar. If not, you can get the required details by contacting the company directly. Most quoted companies have a department that deals exclusively with shareholder and investor queries.

Once you determine who the registrar is, you will usually need to send the following documents to them (but call and check what documents they need before you send anything) in order to have the stock re-issued in the name of the living trust:-

* the original stock certificate relating to the quoted company in question.

* a letter of instruction from you, which is signature guaranteed by a bank, trust company or a brokerage firm registered with the New York Stock Exchange.

* a stock power of attorney, which again is signature guaranteed in the manner described above.

* a copy of your Affidavit of Trust.

As you will need certain documents 'signature guaranteed' you may simply wish to have your broker deal with the transfer on behalf of the living trust. There will invariably be a fee to pay, but it might be the quickest way for you to deal with matters. You will also have the choice of instructing the broker to open an account in the name of the living trust or to have the stocks in question re-issued 'in street name' in their brokerage account – as street accounts are easy to deal with. The choice, however, will be yours.

Did You Know

What does "in street name" mean?

Where the securities and assets of a customer of a brokerage firm are held under the name of the brokerage firm, rather than the name of the customer who purchased those securities and assets, they are said to be held in 'street name'.

If you need to transfer municipal or corporate bonds to your living trust, you can do so in much the same way as outlined above for quoted stock. However, when it comes to 'bearer bonds' you should be aware that the proceeds payable in respect of same will be paid to the person who physically holds such bonds. There will be no formal transfer or registration procedure. It is therefore important to ensure that some record exists of the transfer of those bonds to your living trust. For this reason, you should expressly refer to the bearer bonds in the schedule to your living trust.

Retirement Plans

Due to their complexity, tax advantages and unique distribution features pension plans, profit-sharing plans, IRSs, Keoghs, SEPs and other qualified pension plans should not be transferred into a living trust without first consulting your tax advisor. If the advice received suggests that you can proceed with the transfer, your financial advisor or lawyer should be able to advise you of the transfer formalities.

Life Insurance/Annuities

While the benefit of life insurance policies and annuities can be transferred into a living trust, there is generally no need to do so. In each case, you can designate a specific beneficiary in the policy documentation who will be entitled to receive the proceeds of the insurance or annuity payments when you die. Of course, if you wish, you could name the living trust as the beneficiary so that when you die, the proceeds will be paid directly to the living trust. Once received by the living trust, the successor trustee can distribute those proceeds in whatever manner you have specified in your living trust agreement.

Other Property

If you want to transfer any other property to your living trust, a simple Deed of Assignment (like that contained in the back of this book) should be sufficient to legally effect the transfer. However, if there are specific documents required to transfer specific pieces of property (such as share transfer forms in the case of shares of stock in a corporation) then you should use the required transfer form. If you are uncertain as to the forms you should be using, you should seek the assistance of your attorney.

CHAPTER 10

Executing and Making Changes to Your Living Trust

Executing Your Living Trust

Now that you've had time to think about whether you want to create a living trust and some of the related issues such as who should be your successor trustee, what assets you should transfer to your trust and who should ultimately receive those assets, it's time to start putting a plan in place to create and fund your living trust.

To help you, we have included a number of sample living trust forms at the back of this book. However, before using any of these forms, there are several particularly important steps that you will first need to take. If you do not, you will run the risk on not properly creating or funding your living trust – and we have already touched on the impact that each of these could have.

The relevant steps are set out below. You should feel free to refer to them as often as you wish.

1. Read through this book very carefully. By doing so, you will gain a good overview of living trusts, and will have a much better understanding of how your living trust will work and whether or not a living trust is actually for you.

2. Fill in the Living Trust Worksheet contained at Appendix 1. This is designed to help you compile the information required for inclusion in your living trust agreement. Information regarding your assets, proposed beneficiaries, proposed successor trustees and much more will be gathered in this worksheet. While you may not notice it, as you fill in this worksheet, you will start to make the actual decisions regarding the assets you want to include in your living trust and how you want to ultimately distribute them.

3. Next, you will need to review your own state's legal requirements relating to living trusts. You can do this on the internet. While the standard clauses in our living trust agreements cover many of the potential issues that may arise, there may well be other nuances of state law or factors relating to your personal situation which could impact your decision to use a living trust.

4. Select the form from Appendix 3 which appears most suitable to your circumstances. A copy of the form can be downloaded from the EstateBee website if you prefer. Read through the form carefully. While the form is relatively straight forward, you should never sign a legal document without first reading it in its entirety and fully understanding it. If you are in any doubt as to what something means, contact an attorney.

5. You should carefully follow the procedure and instructions set out in Appendix 2 when filling in the required information in your living trust form. You should use the information in your Living Trust Worksheet to help you with this task.

6. Once completed, proofread your entire living trust agreement to ensure that there are no omissions or typographical errors, and that all provisions are written exactly as you require.

7. To execute your completed living trust agreement, simply follow the procedures set out in Appendix 2.

8. Once executed, you should consider giving a photocopy of your original, signed living trust to your successor trustee as he may need to act under it during any period in which you are incapacitated. Keep the original in a safe place.

That is all there is to it.

Reviewing Your Living Trust

In the same way as you would ordinarily review your finances or health regularly, it is important that you review important legal documents such as your living trust agreement and your last will and testament regularly. We recommend that you carry out this review every year or, at the least every two to three years. In addition, we recommend that you carry out a similar review whenever there is a major change to your personal or financial position – such as in the case of a birth, death or divorce in your family or in the case of a substantial appreciation or depreciation in the value of the trust assets or indeed your own assets.

Depending on the change in question, it may be necessary or desirable to amend the terms of your living trust agreement. Amending your living trust agreement is discussed below.

Amending Your Living Trust Agreement

Important Note

One of the main advantages of a revocable living trust is that you can amend its terms or revoke it at any time. This gives you the flexibility to ensure that its provisions keep pace with changes in your personal circumstances and the circumstances of those who are designated to benefit under the living trust.

The most common reasons why you might want to amend your living trust include: -

- A change in your marital status.
- A move to another state.
- The birth or adoption of a new child.
- A child beneficiary becoming an adult.
- A material change in your financial position or the value of your trust assets.
- A major change in tax law.
- The death of one of your named beneficiaries.
- Your desire to designate a new beneficiary or change existing beneficiaries.
- The death of one of your successor trustees or the making of a decision by one of your successor trustees not to serve.

The occurrence of any of the above events, or indeed any similar event, may lead you to decide to change the terms of your living trust agreement. The process of making these changes is generally quite easy. All you need to do is complete an 'Amendment Agreement'. Like the living trust agreement, the amendment agreement will be made between you as grantor and you as trustee of the living trust. It will usually provide for the deletion of one clause or sentence in your living trust and the inclusion of another clause or clauses in its place. A template Amendment Agreement can be purchased from the EstateBee website www.estate-bee.com.

Resource

Living Trust Amendment Agreement

For a Living Trust Amendment Agreement, simply visit:

www.estate-bee.com/product-category/ legal-forms/revocable-living-trust- forms/

While it is not legally required, we recommend that you have your amendment agreement notarized where it affects the distribution of real estate held within your living trust. This may help address any concerns that documents relating to the transfer of real estate should be notarized.

Transferring and Removing Property from the Trust

We reviewed how you can transfer different types of property to your living trust in the last chapter. These transfer mechanisms can be used when first funding your living trust and when also adding assets to it later. In each case, you sign a transfer document and update the schedule at the back of the trust agreement. Similarly, if you want to remove property held by the trust and transfer it back into your name personally, you will again need to execute a transfer document and update the schedule. However, in this case, you will act in reverse. The living trust will be the transferor and you will be the transferee. In addition, you will also need to remove the transferred property from the schedule at the back of the living trust agreement – rather than adding to it.

Revocation of Your Living Trust

If you want to revoke your living trust at any time, you are free to do so. The process of revoking your trust is straightforward. All you need to do is:

- First, in your capacity as grantor, prepare and serve a notice of revocation of the living trust on yourself as trustee of the trust. This notice will inform the trustee that the trust is terminated and will call for the immediate return of the trust assets to you as grantor. A sample notice of revocation has been included at Appendix 6.

- Secondly, having served a notice of revocation on the trustee, you will need to arrange for the transfer of the legal title in the trust assets to you personally. This will involve the use of the transfer documents we discussed above and in the previous chapter. Again, all transfers will be between you as trustee and you as grantor.

At this juncture, it's useful to again mention that in the case of a shared trust, either grantor acting alone can terminate the living trust and demand the return of all his/her trust assets to him/her. In that case, the grantor terminating the trust would need to serve a notice of termination on each of the two trustees of the trust simultaneously. The trustees will usually be the grantor terminating the living trust and his or her spouse.

In conjunction with the termination of your living trust, it will also be necessary to ensure that any beneficiary designations which you previously made in favor of the living trust are removed or amended. In this respect, we are referring to things such pay-on-death accounts, life insurance policies, etc. This is necessary to ensure that the assets are not transferred to an 'entity' that does not exist and that your overall estate plan remains in 'sync'.

CHAPTER 11

Administering a Living Trust After the Grantor Dies

The Successor Trustee's Role

After you die, your successor trustee will assume control of your living trust and administer it in accordance with the terms of the living trust agreement. This administration process will involve the collection of assets, payment of debts and taxes and the distribution of the trust assets to the beneficiaries named in the living trust agreement. A more detailed examination of that process is set out in the ensuing pages.

Obtaining Certified Copies of the Death Certificate

One of the successor trustee's first tasks following your death will be to obtain copies of your death certificate. The successor trustee will need to present a copy of the certificate, together with an affidavit of trust, to third parties when dealing with the trust assets. Financial institutions, such as banks and life insurance companies, will require both documents before allowing the successor trustee to access any accounts or policies held in the trust's name.

Death certificates can usually be obtained from the state office of vital records or from the department of health, but the precise practice varies a little from state to state. Alternatively, your physician should be able to provide copies of your death certificate to the successor trustee.

Your successor trustee should obtain a number of stamped certified copies of your death certificate as he will generally need to present a certified and sealed original certificate when dealing with financial institutions and carrying out land and real estate transfers. As a rule of thumb, he should get one certificate for each different financial institution he is dealing with as a well as one for each piece of real estate he intends transferring.

Obtaining Tax Identification Number for the Trust

Next, your successor trustee will need to make an application to the IRS to obtain a tax identification number for the living trust. This application should be made using the IRS Form SS-4 or by applying online through www.irs.gov.

In the case of a shared living trust, an application may need to be made for a tax number for each of the two resulting trusts that are created when the first spouse dies. The first trust, being the trust of the deceased spouse, will need a new tax number regardless as it will have become irrevocable. Whether or not the second trust created for the surviving spouse requires a new tax identification number depends on the nature of the trust created. If the successor trustee is also the surviving spouse, and an AB trust has not been created, the successor trustee (surviving spouse) may use his or her social security number as the tax identification number for the second trust. However, if the shared trust was an AB trust or the trustee is someone other than the surviving spouse, a new tax identification number will be required for the second trust also.

Notifying Beneficiaries

The successor trustee will need to notify all the beneficiaries named in the living trust agreement of your death and of the possibility that they may receive a gift under the living trust. In many cases, the obligation to notify beneficiaries is set out within the terms of the living trust agreement itself or under state law. For example, section 7-303 of the Uniform Probate Code provides that:

"the trustee shall keep the beneficiaries of the trust reasonably informed of the trust and its administration. In addition:

(a) *Within 30 days after his acceptance of the trust, the trustee shall inform in writing the current beneficiaries of the Court in which the trust is registered and of his name and address.*

(b) *Upon reasonable request, the trustee shall provide the beneficiary with a copy of the terms of the trust which describe or affect his interest and with relevant information about the assets of the trust and the particulars relating to the administration.*

(c)   *Upon reasonable request, a beneficiary is entitled to a statement of the accounts of the trust annually and on termination of the trust or change of the trustee."*

As can be seen from paragraph (c) above, the successor trustee is not obliged to deliver a set of trust accounts to a trust beneficiary unless that beneficiary has requested a copy of those accounts. The lack of a formal obligation on the part of the successor trustee to deliver trust accounts to all beneficiaries is intended to avoid imposing extensive administrative burdens on the successor trustee. Yet, by requiring the successor trustee to provide the accounts to a beneficiary upon request, the interests of the beneficiary are adequately protected. In most cases, where a beneficiary requests a copy of the trust accounts, the successor trustee will send him a copy of the annual tax returns together with a narrative explaining the movements of trust assets and funds.

Collecting and Managing Trust Assets

Having obtained a death certificate and made an affidavit of trust, the next task for the successor trustee will be to take possession of the trust's assets and to evaluate what debts, claims, taxes and other expenses will be payable by it.

The successor trustee should commence the process by reviewing the trust agreement and trust records to establish what assets have been transferred to your living trust and what debts might exist. Once he has completed this exercise and spoken to the executor of your estate if necessary, and if he has not done so already, he will need to secure the trust assets to ensure that their value is maintained.

Assets and legal documents such as securities (especially bearer bonds), title deeds, jewelry, and other items of substantial value should be placed in a safe deposit box (in the trust's name) or safe. Other assets such as real estate, vehicles and 'personal property' of value should be adequately insured against risks such as fire, damage, theft, loss, and liability, as appropriate. In this regard, the successor trustee will need to contact the relevant insurance companies to ensure that your death has not caused any of the existing policies (which should have been registered in the name of the living trust and not your personal name) to lapse. If any of the policies have lapsed or if it transpires than some or all of the trust assets were not covered by an insurance policy, your successor trustee will need to organize for appropriate insurance cover to be put in place.

Once the existing assets are secured, the successor trustee will need to consider whether there are any other assets which the trust is entitled to claim. If there are, he will need to take appropriate steps to ensure that they are taken under his possession and/or control.

Claiming Life Insurance Proceeds

The successor trustee should contact each insurance company with whom you held a policy of life insurance. If the living trust was named as a designated beneficiary of any of these policies, the successor trustee will need to make appropriate applications to have the proceeds of those policies released to the living trust. As mentioned, the insurance company will most likely require the successor trustee to provide it with a copy of your death certificate as well as a completed affidavit of trust before dealing with the successor trustee. In addition, it may also require the successor trustee to fill out certain standard claim forms. Once these documents have been completed and received by the insurance company, the claim can be processed, and the funds released to the living trust. Once the insurance proceeds are received by the trust, they should be placed into a federally insured trust account pending subsequent release to the trust beneficiaries.

Accessing Bank Accounts & Other Financial Accounts

The next step for the successor trustee will be to notify each financial institution which held an account in the name of the trust of your death and can commence the process of having the proceeds of those accounts released to his control. Again, like insurance companies, the financial institutions will require copies of your death certificate and an affidavit of trust. Once the funds are released, the proceeds should be transferred into a federally insured trust account.

Identifying Debts Owed by the Grantor

The successor trustee will need to examine the records relating to the living trust and your affairs generally so as to ensure that all of the debts owing by the trust and by you personally at the time of your death are discharged. As mentioned, personal debts owing by you at the time of your death will normally be discharged from your personal estate rather than your trust estate. These debts might include mortgages, credit cards, utility bills, personal loans, car loans, etc.

Maintaining Proper Accountings of Trust Assets

As mentioned earlier in this book, a successor trustee will be under a duty to prepare an annual accounting in respect of the trust assets. Whether or not the successor trustee will need to supply that accounting to the beneficiaries will depend on several factors. In certain cases, as mentioned, state law can oblige the successor trustee to furnish the accounting only where requested to do so by a beneficiary. In other cases, the terms of a living trust agreement may expressly provide that there will be no obligation on the successor trustee to do so. In further cases, the beneficiaries can waive their entitlement to receive an accounting. Your successor trustee should, therefore, carefully review the terms of your living trust agreement and the relevant sections of state law before incurring the time and cost of sending accountings to beneficiaries.

Where an accounting is prepared, it should include a description of the assets held by the trust as well as details of the current market valuations of those assets. It should also include details of any income received, any expenditure made, and any assets added to or taken out of the trust during the relevant accounting period. To facilitate the preparation of these accounts, the successor trustee will need to keep meticulous records of all transactions involving the trust. For this reason, it is often recommended that moneys be pooled in a single account in the trust's name and that all monies be distrusted by means of a bank transfer or check so that there is a clear audit trail of all transactions carried out by the successor trustee on behalf of the trust.

Finally, to determine the market value of the trust assets requiring valuations, the successor trustee may need to engage the services of professional valuation agents such as stockbrokers, realtors, etc. The preparation of these valuations will be important for the purpose of determining the level of federal estate tax, if any, that may be owed by your estate following your death. Again, as the living trust is transparent for tax purposes, your successor trustee will need to work closely with the executor of your estate in order to obtain a combined market valuation for all of your assets (inside and outside of the living trust) at the date of your death.

Preparing and Filing Tax Returns

The successor trustee and the executor of your estate will be collectively responsible for ensuring that all taxes due by you at the time of your death are paid. In this regard, there will be several specific taxes which may be due and owing by you and these are discussed separately below.

Federal Estate Tax

To determine the amount of federal estate taxes owing by you at the time of your death, the extent and value of your estate both inside and outside of your living trust will need to be ascertained. If the value of that combined estate exceeds the federal estate tax threshold applicable at the time of your death (it's $11.7 million for those who die in 2021), estate tax will become payable at the rate of 40% on the excess (or whatever amount is applicable when you die). It is the responsibility of both your executor and successor trustee to determine if any estate tax is due by your estate and, if so, to make an appropriate tax return. The executor and successor trustee will have a period of nine months from the date of your death to file the tax return and to discharge any estate taxes that are due. An extension of six months may be obtained in certain circumstances.

Income Taxes

Final income tax returns will also need to be made in the year of your death. This return should be made in your name using IRS Form 1040. Like the payment of federal estate tax, the payment of this tax should be coordinated with the executor as it should be made by your estate in the first instance. It is only if there are insufficient assets in the estate to meet the payment that the trust should be called upon to make the required payment.

Trust Income Tax Returns

After your death, your successor trustee will need to submit details of all income generated by the living trust to the IRS. This submission should be made in each calendar year using IRS Form 1041. It will be the sole responsibility of your successor trustee to ensure that these returns are made.

Remember, that if your living trust is a shared trust and splits into two separate trusts on the death of you or your spouse, two separate tax returns will need to be made. The deceased spouse's trust will need to make the return under its own tax number using IRS Form 1041. If the surviving spouse is the sole trustee of the surviving spouse's trust and the trust is not an AB trust, then the surviving trustee will need to file tax returns for the trust under his or her tax identification number using IRS Form 1040. However, if the living trust is an AB trust or the trustee of the surviving spouse's resulting trust is not the surviving spouse, the appropriate returns should be made under the resulting trust's own tax number on an IRS Form 1041.

State Taxes and Pick-Up Taxes

Finally, the executor of your estate and your successor trustee will also need to ensure that any state taxes or pick-up taxes owing by your estate are discharged. For more information on these charges, see Chapter 8.

Transferring Property to Beneficiaries

Once all the assets have been collected in and all debts and taxes paid or provided for, the successor trustee can distribute the remaining trust assets in accordance with the terms of the living trust agreement. The assets will either be distributed (i) in cash if the gift is in cash or if the trust assets have been converted to cash or (ii) in kind if the trust included tangible assets.

In order to properly distribute the trust assets to the beneficiaries, your successor trustee will need to re-register the trust assets in the names of the relevant beneficiaries and, where necessary, deliver up possession and control of the assets in question. In dealing with the re-registration of ownership of the assets, the successor trustee will need to go through the process for transferring title in the trust assets over to the beneficiaries. This process has been outlined Chapter 9.

When transferring trust assets to the beneficiaries, the successor trustee should ensure that each beneficiary signs a form of written acknowledgement to confirm that he or she has received the asset in question. This can either take the form of the transfer document itself (where legal transfers are required) or simply a written statement acknowledging receipt (in the case of a cash gift or the gift of an item which does not require the use of a specific form of transfer, such as jewelry or a painting).

Administering a Child's Trust

The duties of a successor trustee will normally terminate once he has distributed all the trust assets to the beneficiaries named in the trust agreement. However, if a sub-trust has been created under the terms of that agreement for the benefit of a young beneficiary, the successor trustee will need to continue acting as trustee of that sub-trust. This means that he will need to continue managing the assets in the sub-trust until such time as the young beneficiary or beneficiaries (if there is more than one) reach an age specified in the trust agreement.

The management of the sub-trust(s) will greatly add to the duties and tasks of the successor trustee. In particular, he will need to ensure that the sub-trust assets are properly invested and secured for the period of the sub-trust; as well as make provisions during that time for the welfare, upkeep and education of the young beneficiary. Only when the last beneficiary reaches the age specified in the trust agreement can the successor trustee formally distribute the remaining trust assets and wind down the living trust. This may well be years or even decades after your death. Of course, the trust can be wound up sooner if the trust assets are depleted in full before the beneficiary reaches the age of termination specified in the trust agreement or if the beneficiary dies.

Conclusion

The length of time that it takes to settle the trust and distribute assets is often dependent on whether any estate tax is payable by the grantor. If a return is due, it is usually prudent to delay making final distributions until after a closing letter has been received from the IRS confirming all taxes due by your estate have been paid. While this normally only takes a few months, if there are difficulties in determining the value of your estate, or other tax issues, the process can take up to 18 months to complete. Similar delays will arise if your estate is audited. However, if no federal estate tax is due, the trust can usually be wound up within a few months; assuming of course that no child trusts have been established under the terms of the living trust agreement.

CHAPTER 12

Ancillary Estate Planning Documents

What Is a 'Pour-Over Will?'

A pour-over will is a special type of will that is used in conjunction with a living trust. Instead of providing for the distribution of all of your assets and property following your death, a pour-over will simply provides for the transfer of any property that you have not already transferred to your living trust at the time of your death to your living trust. This ensures that all your assets can be distributed in accordance with the provisions of your living trust agreement.

A pour-over will resembles normal wills in many ways. It provides for the revocation of other wills, names an executor, and appoints a guardian for minor children. The one real difference is that there is usually only one beneficiary – your living trust.

While a pour-over will has certain advantages, the major drawback is that the assets passing under your will still have to go through probate (or one of the streamlined alternatives for small estates). As such, probate of your estate will usually need to complete before those assets are received by the living trust. Once received, the beneficiaries named in the living trust agreement will have to wait for a further period for the successor trustee to make the required distributions from the living trust. The chances of a speedy distribution in those circumstances can be slim unless your estate is small enough to avail of the expedited procedures available for the probate of 'small estates'. For more information on this, see Chapter 2.

However, the use of a pour-over will can be beneficial where circumstances exist which deter people from putting all their property into living trusts during their lifetimes. For example, the laws in certain states and the policies of certain insurance companies impose restrictions on the abilities of people to buy, sell, or insure assets held in a living trust. For this reason, these assets are often left outside of the trust until you die. After your death, assets are often transferred to your living trust via the probate process.

In other situations, people who have established living trusts simply forget to transfer all their assets to the trust or do not get an opportunity to do so before they die. For example, you could receive an inheritance of land a few days before you die and simply never get an opportunity during your last days to make the required transfer.

The use of a pour-over will is therefore a good means to avoid intestacy and having state law determine how your assets will be distributed following your death. All that said, there is no reason why you can't include a residuary clause in your will that mirrors that contained in your living trust agreement as it more or less accomplishes the same thing. However, if you gift some or all of the residuary trust estate to a child under your living trust, you may want the non-trust estate assets to be transferred to the living trust so that the successor trustee can administer everything under one trust rather than having to create a second under your will. In such circumstances, it may make sense to allow the excess assets from your estate to flow into your living trust.

In summary, it is fair to say that if you set up a living trust you will also need a will. Whether the terms of that will should provide specifically for the distribution of property or whether it should provide for the pour-over of that property to your living trust is a matter of personal choice.

Did You Know

When it comes to estate planning, a **last will and testament** is one of the most important documents you can have. In many cases, it will operate in tandem with your living trust by 'pouring' certain assets of your personal estate into your living trust when you die. In addition, it allows you to appoint guardians for your children and reduce the risk of creditors suing your estate or your living trust to recover debts owed to them. So, do not make the mistake of thinking that having a living trust replaces the need to have a last will – that is not the case at all, **you need both**.

Did You Know

Equally important, is the need to have a **durable general power of attorney** which allows your designated agent deal with your property if you become incapacitated. Remember, while the incapacity provisions in a living trust allow your successor trustee to manage the trust assets if you become incapacitated, they do not allow him to deal with assets that have not been transferred to the trust. This is where a durable power of attorney comes in.

Avoiding Conflicts between Your Living Trust & Your Will

If you set up a living trust and create a will, you will need to carefully review the terms of each to ensure that there is not conflict between them. For example, you will want to avoid a situation where you leave your favorite painting to two different people – one gift being made under your living trust, the other being made under your living trust. If this happens, a careful review of the documents relating to the transfer of the painting to the living trust will invariably follow to establish whether the painting was properly transferred to the trust. The ownership of the painting will determine who has the right to gift it – you or the trust.

For the above reasons, it is a good idea to update your will every time you transfer assets to your living trust.

Warning

If you live in Washington state, be careful. Washington state law provides that if there is a conflict between the terms of your will and your living trust, the provisions of your living trust will prevail over those in your will. As such, taking the above example, the person named in your will could become entitled to the painting while the person named in your living trust could miss out.

Planning for Incapacity – Power of Attorney for Finance & Property

A power of attorney is a legal document by which you can appoint and authorize another person (usually a trusted friend, family member, colleague or adviser) to act on your behalf in the event that you are unable to act yourself due to incapacity or otherwise.

There are two principal types of powers of attorney, an ordinary power of attorney and a durable power of attorney. Ordinary powers of attorney automatically come to an end if you become incapacitated. Durable powers of attorney, by contrast, do not come to an end if you become incapacitated and, in many cases, often only commence at such time. For this reason, durable powers of attorney are typically used for estate planning purposes.

Durable powers of attorney come in two forms – a durable general power of attorney and a durable limited power of attorney. Under a durable general power of attorney, your appointed agent will be authorized to act as your legal representative in relation to all your legal and financial affairs. In other words, your agent will acting in your name and on your behalf, be able to collect and disburse money; operate your bank accounts; buy and sell property; refurbish and rent out your property; and generally sign documents and deeds.

The authorization under a power of attorney will usually commence on the date specified in the document or, more commonly, on the date that you are determined to be incapacitated. The authorization will end when you revoke it (which, in the case of incapacity, you can only do if you regain capacity) or die.

While the law varies from state to state, a person will usually be deemed to be 'incapable' or 'incapacitated' if they are either (i) unable to understand and process information that is relevant to making an informed decision and (ii) unable to evaluate the likely consequences of making that decision. In many cases, the procedure for determining whether a person is incapacitated is set out in the power of attorney document itself and typically involves assessments by medical physicians.

Resource

Make Your Own Medical & Financial Powers of Attorney

Powers of attorney allow people you trust to manage your property and financial affairs during periods in which you are incapacitated; as well as make medical decisions on your behalf based on the instructions in your power of attorney document. This ensures that your affairs do not go unmanaged if you are incapacitated and you do not receive any unwanted medical treatments.

This book provides all the necessary documents and step-by-step instructions to make a power of attorney to cover virtually any situation. Get your copy at **www.estate-bee.com/product/make-your-own-medical-financial-powers-of-attorney**

The second type of durable power of attorney is a durable limited power of attorney. This is like a durable general power of attorney except that it expressly limits the agent's authority to act on your behalf. In this regard, you can set out exactly what the agent can do and what he cannot. For example, you might authorize him to deal with a particular business you own and nothing else. The choice is yours.

If you fail to make a power of attorney, your family may have to formally apply to court to have a guardian or conservator appointed to manage your legal and financial affairs. This person, who may or may not be a family member, will have power to make decisions on your behalf and generally to manage your affairs as he sees fit – without regard to your wishes or those of your family. Of course, the situation can be avoided by having a power of attorney.

In broad terms, the general view is that, (i) the more complex and sensitive your affairs are, (ii) the higher the standard of living your family is accustomed to, and/or (iii) the more disruptive any disability to perform on your part would be — the greater the need to make a power of attorney to protect your assets and provide for your family.

Planning for Incapacity – Advance Healthcare Directives

Advance healthcare directives enable you to instruct others about the medical care you would like to receive if you are unable to make decisions for yourself or communicate those decisions. There are two specific types of healthcare directives to consider, each with differing features. These are living wills and healthcare powers of attorney.

Living Wills

A living will is a legal document that allows you to instruct healthcare providers in relation to the use or non-use of certain life-sustaining medical treatments in the event that you are terminally ill or permanently unconscious and unable to communicate your own wishes.

To understand the uses of a living will, it is useful to define some medical terms:

- *Life-sustaining medical treatment* means any form of healthcare that will serve mainly to prolong or delay the process of dying.

- *Terminal illness* or *terminal condition* means an irreversible, incurable, and untreatable condition caused by disease, illness, or injury.

- *Permanently unconscious* means an irreversible condition in which you are permanently unaware of yourself and your surroundings.

- *Comfort care* or *palliative care* means any measure taken to diminish pain or discomfort, but not to postpone death.

You can use a living will to set out your preferences in relation to the receipt or non-receipt of nutrition, hydration, blood, CPR, mechanical respiration, and much more. However, even where you have a living will, healthcare personnel will still provide comfort care to you. They generally will not stand by and leave you in severe physical pain, for example.

Resource

Healthcare Power of Attorney & Living Will Kit

This Healthcare Power of Attorney & Living Will Kit allows you to appoint an agent to make medical decisions on your behalf if you are unconscious or otherwise unable to do so yourself. It also allows you to set out your preferences regarding the receipt or non-receipt of life sustaining medical treatments during any period in which you are permanently unconscious or suffering from a terminal illness and unable to communicate your wishes.

This Kit contains all the information and ready-to-use lawyer prepared legal forms and documents necessary to create a combined Healthcare Power of Attorney and Living Will. Get your copy at **www.estate-bee. com/product/helathcare-power-of-attorney-living-will-kit/**

The way a living will works is quite straightforward. In most states, two doctors must agree that the use of medical procedures will only prolong the dying process and that, absent the use of such procedures, death would occur in the short term. If both doctors agree that this is the case, then the medical procedures may be withdrawn or withheld, depending on the contents of the living will.

Other names for living wills include 'instructions', 'directive to physicians' and 'declaration'.

Healthcare Power of Attorney

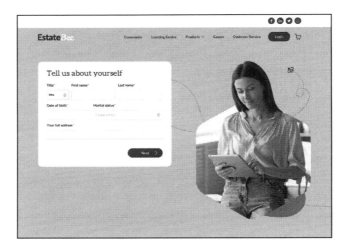

Make Your Power of Attorney Online

If you wish to create a power of attorney, we recommend using EstateBee's online power of attorney software as it contains a number of flexible options that cannot reasonably be catered for in 'fill-in-the-blank' type documents. For more information visit **www.estate-bee.com/product/online-power-of-attorney/**

Two of the principal limitations of living wills is that they only (i) become effective when you are terminally ill, or permanently unconscious, and unable to communicate your wishes and (ii) deal with the receipt of life sustaining treatments – as opposed to any other kind of treatments.

On the other hand, a healthcare power of attorney allows you to appoint someone (an agent) to make all kinds of medical decisions for you irrespective of whether you are terminally ill or permanently unconscious. The agent's authority will usually only become effective once your attending physician determines that you have lost the capacity to make informed healthcare decisions. For so long as you have the capacity to make your own decisions, you retain the right to make all your own medical and healthcare decisions.

The authority of your agent to make healthcare decisions for you generally includes the authority to give informed consent; refuse to give informed consent; or withdraw informed consent for any care, treatment, service, or procedure designed to maintain, diagnose, or treat a physical or mental condition. However, you can expressly limit your agent's authority under a power of attorney if you wish.

Conclusion

The above are only samples of the additional documents which ought to be included in any comprehensive estate plan. For more information on any of these documents or on estate planning generally, visit www.estate-bee.com.

Appendices

Appendix 1

Living Trust Worksheet

Downloadable Forms

Blank copies of this worksheet can be downloaded from the EstateBee website. Simply login to your account or, if you do not have an account, you can create one for free.

www.estate-bee.com/login

Once logged in, go to your profile page and enter the code listed below in the 'Use Codes' tab:

LTAAB129LTB

Living Trust Worksheet

Before you begin the process of making a living trust, we recommend that you print out this worksheet and complete it as appropriate. It will help you to work out what assets you actually own, and identify your liabilities, before deciding what assets you would like to transfer to your living trust and who you would like to make gifts to and how. By having all the relevant details at your fingertips, it will save a considerable amount of time in the preparation of your living trust.

The document is also useful for documenting your choice of fiduciaries such as executors, trustees, healthcare agents, etc.

In addition, by keeping this worksheet with your living trust, last will, and other personal papers, it will greatly assist your trustees and executors in identifying and locating your assets and liabilities when the time comes.

Personal Information	You	Your Spouse
Full Name:		
Birth Date:		
Social Security Number:		
Occupation:		
Work Telephone:		
Work Fax:		
Mobile/Pager:		
Email Address:		
Home Address (Include County):		
Home Telephone:		
Home Fax:		

Date and Place of Marriage:	
Maiden name of Spouse:	

If either of you were previously married, list the dates of prior marriage, name of previous spouse, names of living children from prior marriage(s), and state whether marriage ended by death or divorce:		
Location of Safe Deposit Box (if any):		

Notification of Death

(On my death, please notify the following persons)

Full Name	Telephone	Address

Children (Living)		
Full Name	Address (if the child does not reside with you)	Birth Date

Children (Deceased)		
Full Name		

Grandchildren		
Full Name	Address	Birth Date

Parents		
Full Name	Address	Telephone Number

Brothers and Sisters		
Full Name	Address	Telephone Number

Assets		
Description & Location	Current Fair Market Value	How is Title Held?
Real Estate (Land and Buildings)		

Closely Held Companies, Businesses, Partnerships etc.		
Bank Accounts		
Shares, Bonds and Mutual Funds		
Vehicles, Boats, etc		

Other Property		
Total		

Liabilities		
Description		Amount
Mortgages		
Loans		

Debts	
Other Liabilities	
Total	

Life Insurance and Annuities				
Company	Insured	Beneficiary(ies)	Face Amount	Cash Value
Total				

Pensions and Other Retirement Plans				
Company Custodian	Participant	Type of Plan	Vested Amount	Death Benefit
Total				

Distribution Plan
(Describe in general terms how you wish to leave your property at death)

Other Beneficiaries

(Information about persons other than your spouse and family members who you wish to benefit)

Full Name	Age	Address	Relationship to You

Fiduciaries

(List name, address and home telephone for each person)

	Full Name	Address	Telephone Number
Last Will and Testament			
Primary Executor:			
First Alternate Executor:			
Second Alternate Executor:			

Primary Trustee:			
First Alternate Trustee:			
Second Alternate Trustee:			
Guardian of Minor Children:			
First Alternate Guardian:			
Second Alternate Guardian:			
Living Trust			
Successor Trustee:			
First Alternate Successor Trustee:			
Second Alternate Successor Trustee:			
Agent under a Power of Attorney for Finance and Property			
Agent:			
First Alternate Agent:			
Second Alternate Agent:			
Agent under a Healthcare Power of Attorney			
Healthcare Agent:			

First Alternate Healthcare Agent:			
Second Alternate Healthcare Agent:			
Living Will			
Healthcare Agent:			
First Alternate Healthcare Agent:			
Second Alternate Healthcare Agent:			

Advisors
(List name, address and home telephone for each person)

	Full Name	Address	Telephone Number
Lawyer			
Accountant			
Financial Advisor			
Stockbroker			
Insurance Agent			
Other Information:			

Document Locations		
Description	Location	Other Information
Last Will & Testament		
Trust Agreement		
Living Will		
Healthcare Power of Attorney		
Power of Attorney for Finance and Property		
Title Deeds		
Leases		
Share Certificates		
Mortgage Documents		
Birth Certificate		
Marriage Certificate		
Divorce Decree		
Donor Cards		

Other Documents	

Funeral Plan

(Describe in general terms what funeral and burial arrangements you would like to have)

Appendix 2

Instructions for Completing Your Documents

Revocable Living Trust for an Individual

1. On the cover page, insert the date of execution of the Agreement as well as your name as both grantor and trustee in the spaces provided. Remember, as you will act as both grantor and trustee, the agreement will be between you (as grantor) and you (as trustee).

2. On page 1, enter the date of execution of the Agreement at the very top of the Agreement.

3. The top half of page one identifies the parties to the agreement. You should enter your name and address in the spaces provided for insertion in (1) and (2) (details of both the grantor and trustee respectively).

4. At clause 1.1, insert details of the name of the trust. For example, if your name is John Smith, it is common to name the trust as "the John Smith Revocable Living Trust". Adopting this approach, just enter your name in the space provided.

5. In clause 4, you will instruct your successor trustee as to what gifts should be made and to whom on your death. In this clause, there are two types of gifts – specific gifts and gifts of the residuary trust estate.

Specific Gifts

You are not obliged to make any specific gifts. In fact, you can have as many specific gifts as you like or even none – the choice is yours. Depending on your preference in this respect, you will need to add or delete specific gift clauses from your agreement but remember to adjust the numbering in the clause accordingly.

To complete a standard gift clause, simply insert the name and address of the beneficiary into the gift clause together with details of what that beneficiary is to receive from the trust estate. If you wish to appoint an alternate beneficiary who will receive this gift if the primary beneficiary dies before you, you can do so. Simply, refer to Appendix 4 for an appropriate clause which can be substituted for the default clause in the agreement. Remember, there is no obligation on you to appoint an alternate beneficiary for a specific gift. If the primary beneficiary dies before you, and no alternate beneficiary is appointed the asset gifted to him/her under the agreement will revert to form part of the residuary trust estate.

Residuary Trust Estate

You must complete the gift of the residuary estate in all circumstances.

You can name one primary beneficiary and one or more alternates OR multiple primary beneficiaries and multiple alternates. The clause for a single primary beneficiary and a single alternate beneficiary is included by default in this agreement. If you wish to change this to multiple primary beneficiaries and/or multiple alternate beneficiaries, simply replace the default clause in the agreement with the relevant clause from Appendix 4.

To complete the residuary gift clause for a single primary beneficiary and single alternate beneficiary, simply insert the name and address of both the primary beneficiary and the alternate beneficiary in the spaces provided.

You can complete the residuary gift clause for multiple primary beneficiaries and multiple alternate beneficiaries in the same way as mentioned in the previous paragraph. However, in addition to the above, you will also need to specify what percentage of the overall trust estate each primary beneficiary is to receive. The total must of course equal 100%. Also, you must specify what percentage of the primary beneficiary's interest each alternate beneficiary is to receive. Remember, that the alternates should be allocated 100% of the primary beneficiary's interest of the trust estate.

Simple Note: Primary beneficiaries receive a % interest in the trust estate. They must be allocated 100% in total between them.

Alternate beneficiaries receive a % interest in the primary beneficiary's share of the trust estate...not an interest in the trust estate directly.

100% of the primary beneficiary's share should be divided between the alternates.

Example 1: 20% thereof shall be given to Primary Beneficiary No 1 of Small Town, Big County, New York. If this person shall fail to survive the Grantor, his/her share of the Residue Trust Estate shall be given to Alternate Beneficiary No 1 of Small Town, Big County, New York.

Example 2: 80% thereof shall be given to Primary Beneficiary No 2 of Small Town, Big County, New York. If this person shall fail to survive the Grantor, his/her share of the Residue Trust Estate shall be divided by the Successor Trustee as follows:

    (i)   60% thereof shall be given to Alternate Beneficiary No 2 of Small Town, Big County, New York.

    (ii)   40% thereof shall be given to Alternate Beneficiary No 3 of Small Town, Big County, New York.

6. In clause 7.1, insert the name and address of both your successor trustee and your alternate successor trustee.

7. At clause, 9.3 specify the state in which you are resident. The laws of this state will govern the operation of the trust.

8. On the execution page of the agreement, you should sign the agreement as both grantor and trustee in the presence of two witnesses. Your witnesses should each write their names and sign their names in the spaces provided.

9. In the schedule, you should insert details of all the assets you are transferring to your revocable living trust. Remember, if the assets have title documents and a prescribed means by which they should be transferred, you should ensure that the transfer is carried out correctly. If there is no prescribed transfer document, but the transfer document is required you can use the deed of assignment contained in this kit. If you are in any doubt as to what document should be used to effect the transfer, speak to an attorney.

   If no transfer document is required, simply add details of the asset in the schedule at the back of the agreement.

10. The final page of the agreement contains a notary affidavit. There is generally no requirement that you have a notary complete this affidavit. However, we recommend that you have it completed as it lessens the likelihood that your execution of the trust agreement could be challenged by others. Simply bring the agreement together with identification to a notary and he or she will be able to assist you with the rest.

Note: If you wish to add any property management provisions, see Appendix 4. The relevant clause should be added at clause 5 of the trust agreement.

Revocable Living Trust for a Couple and AB Revocable Living Trust for a Couple

1. On the cover page, insert the date of execution of the Agreement as well as the names of both grantors and trustees in the spaces provided. Remember, as you and your spouse will act as both grantors and trustees, the agreement will be between you and your spouse (as grantors) and you and your spouse (as trustees).

2. On page 1, enter the date of execution of the Agreement at the very top of the Agreement.

3. The top half of page one identifies the parties to the agreement. You should enter your name and address and your spouse's name and address in the spaces provided in (1) and (2) (details of both the grantors and trustees respectively).

4. At rectal A, enter the husband's name.

5. At recital B, enter the wife's name.

6. At recital C, enter the name of the husband and then the wife.

7. At clause 1.1, insert details of the name of the trust. For example, if your name is John Smith and your wife is Mary Smith, it is common to name the trust as "the John and Mary Smith Revocable Living Trust".

8. At clause 2.4(i), enter the husband's name.

9. At clause 2.4(ii), enter the wife's name.

10. At clause 2.4(iii), enter the name of the husband and then the wife.

11. At clause 3.1.1(a), enter the husband's name.

12. At clause 3.1.1(b), enter the wife's name.

13. At clause 3.1.3(a), enter the husband's name.

14. At clause 3.1.3(b), enter the wife's name.

15. At 4.6.1, enter the husband's name in both spaces. Then specify what gifts you would like to make from the husband's share of the trust assets. Remember, the husband will own the assets in schedule 1 and have an interest in the assets in schedule 3.

   There are three specific gift clauses in this section. Specific gifts of an asset, specific gifts of an interest in an asset and gifts of the residue of the husband's estate. We will discuss each in turn.

Husband's Specific Gifts of Assets (Schedule 1)

The husband is not obliged to make any specific gifts from his share of the trust estate.

In fact, he can have as many specific gifts as he likes or even none – the choice is his. Depending on the preference in this respect, you will need to add or delete specific gift clauses from your agreement but remember to adjust the numbering in the clause accordingly.

To complete a standard gift clause, simply insert the name and address of the beneficiary into the gift clause together with details of what that beneficiary is to receive from the husband's trust estate. If you wish to appoint an alternate beneficiary who will receive this gift if the primary beneficiary dies before the husband, you can do so. Simply, refer to Appendix 4 for an appropriate clause which can be substituted for the default clause in this agreement. Remember, there is no obligation to appoint an alternate beneficiary for a specific gift. If the primary beneficiary dies before the husband, and no alternate beneficiary is appointed, the asset gifted to him/her under the agreement will revert to form part of the husband's residuary trust estate.

Husband's Specific Gifts of an Interest in Assets (Schedule 3)

This clause is completed in much the same way as a specific gift of an asset and it too can contain provisions for an alternate beneficiary. The only addition is that, in completing the clause, the husband's name must be entered into the clause after the name and address of the beneficiary and before the details of the relevant asset. See the example below for an illustration: -

(i)   [Primary Beneficiary Name] of [Primary Beneficiary Address] shall be given [Husband's Name]'s interest in [Details of Asset].

Gift of Husbands Residuary Estate

You must complete the gift of the husband's residuary trust estate in all circumstances.

You can name one primary beneficiary and one or more alternate beneficiaries OR multiple primary beneficiaries and multiple alternates. The clause for a single primary beneficiary and a single alternate beneficiary is included by default in this agreement.

If you wish to change this to multiple primary beneficiaries and/or multiple alternate beneficiaries, simply replace the default clause in the agreement with the relevant clause from Appendix 4.

To complete the residuary gift clause for a single primary beneficiary and single alternate beneficiary, simply insert the name and address of both the primary beneficiary and the alternate beneficiary in the spaces provided. You will also need to insert the husband's name in the relevant places. See completed example below: -

(i)   Any of [Husband Name]'s Trust Estate not otherwise disposed of hereunder ("**[Husband Name]'s Residue Trust Estate**") shall be given to [Primary Beneficiary Name] of [Primary Beneficiary Address] for his/her own use and benefit absolutely. If the aforementioned person predeceases [Husband Name] then in that event his/her share of [Husband Name]'s Residue Trust Estate shall be given to [Alternate Beneficiary Name] of [Alternate Beneficiary Address].

You can complete the residuary gift clause for multiple primary beneficiaries and multiple alternate beneficiaries in the same way as mentioned in the previous paragraph.

However, in addition to the above, you will also need to specify what percentage of the husband's overall trust estate each primary beneficiary is to receive. The total must of course equal 100%. Also, you must specify what percentage of the primary beneficiary's interest each alternate beneficiary is to receive. Remember, that the alternates should be allocated 100% of the primary beneficiary's interest in the husband's trust estate.

Simple Note: Primary beneficiaries receive a % interest in the husband's trust estate.

They must be allocated 100% in total between them. Alternate beneficiaries receive a % interest in the primary beneficiaries' share of the husband's trust estate...not an interest in the husband's trust estate directly. 100% of the primary beneficiary's share should be divided between the alternates.

Example: Any of [Husband Name]'s Trust Estate not otherwise disposed of hereunder ("[Husband Name]'s Residue Trust Estate") shall be divided by the Successor Trustee as follows:

(i)   20% thereof shall be given to [Primary Beneficiary 1 Name] of [Primary Beneficiary 1 Address]. If the aforementioned person shall fail to survive [Husband Name], his/her share of [Husband Name]'s Residue Trust Estate shall be divided by the Successor Trustee as follows:

   a.   60% thereof shall be given to [Alternate Beneficiary 1 Name] of [Alternate Beneficiary 1 Address].

   b.   40% thereof shall be given to [Alternate Beneficiary 2 Name] of [Alternate Beneficiary 2 Address].

(ii)   80% thereof shall be given to [Primary Beneficiary 2 Name] of [Primary Beneficiary 2 Address]. If the aforementioned person shall fail to survive [Husband Name], his/her share of [Husband Name]'s Residue Trust Estate shall be divided by the Successor Trustee as follows:

   a.   50% thereof shall be given to [Alternate Beneficiary 3 Name] of [Alternate Beneficiary 3 Address].

      b.   50% thereof shall be given to [Alternate Beneficiary 3 Name] of [Alternate Beneficiary 3 Address].

16. Clause 4.6.2, the wife's gifts, should be completed in a manner like that set out at point 15 above in respect of the distribution of the husband's gifts. Of course, the wife is free to choose her own beneficiaries. The reference to husband should be considered to be to wife and the reference to Schedule 1 should be considered to be Schedule 2.

17. In clause 8.1 (clause 9.1 in AB Living Trust), insert the name and address of both your successor trustee and your alternate successor trustee.

18. At clause 10.3 (clause 11.3 in AB Living Trust), specify the state in which you are resident. The laws of this state will govern the operation of the trust.

19. On the execution page of the agreement, both the husband and wife should sign the agreement as both grantor and trustee in the presence of two witnesses. Both husband and wife will therefore each need to sign twice. Your witness should each write their names and sign their names in the spaces provided.

20. In the schedules, you should insert details of all the assets being transferred to the revocable living trust. Details of the husband's solely owned assets should be included in Schedule 1. Details of the wife's solely owned assets should be included in Schedule 2. Details of the assets owned jointly by both spouses should be included in Schedule 3.

    Remember, if the assets have title documents and a prescribed means by which they should be transferred, you should ensure that the transfer is carried out correctly. If there is no prescribed transfer document but a transfer document is required, you can use the deed of assignment contained at the back of this kit. If you are in any doubt as to what document should be used to effect the transfer, speak to an attorney.

21. The final page of the agreement contains a notary affidavit. There is generally no requirement that you have a notary complete this affidavit. However, we recommend that you have it completed as it lessens the likelihood that the execution of the trust agreement could be challenged by others. Simply bring the agreement together with identification to a notary and he or she will be able to assist you with the rest. Both you and your spouse should attend.

Note: If you wish to add any property management provisions, see Appendix 4. The relevant clause should be added at clause 5 of the trust agreement.

Deed of Assignment for Use with a Revocable Living Trust for an Individual

1.   On the cover page, insert the date of execution of the deed as well as your name as both grantor and trustee in the spaces provided. Remember, as you are acting as both grantor and trustee, the deed will be between you (as grantor) and you (as trustee).

2.   On page 1, enter the date of execution of the deed at the very top of the page.

3.   The top half of page one identifies the parties to the deed. You should enter your name and address in the spaces provided for insertion in (1) and (2) (details of both the grantor and trustee respectively).

4.   In Recital A, enter the date of creation of the trust and the name of the trust.

5.   At clause 1.1, insert details of the assets you wish to transfer by deed of assignment to the trust. Remember to be as specific as possible in describing the assets.

6.   Print your name in the execution block on the last page and sign your name directly opposite the execution block in the space provided. You should sign your name in the presence of a witness. The witness should print and sign his/her name in the spaces provided under your execution block.

Deed of Assignment for Use with a Revocable Living Trust for a Couple

1.   On the cover page, insert the date of execution of the deed as well as your name and that of your spouse as both grantors and trustees in the spaces provided. Remember, as you and your spouse are grantors and trustees, the deed will be between you and your spouse (as grantors) and you and your spouse (as trustees).

2.   On page 1, enter the date of execution of the deed at the very top of the page.

3. The top half of page one identifies the parties to the deed. You should enter your name and address and your spouse's name and address in the spaces provided for insertion in (1) and (2) (details of both the grantors and trustees respectively).

4. In Recital A, enter the date of creation of the trust and the name of the trust.

5. At clause 1.1, insert details of the assets you wish to transfer by deed of assignment to the trust. Remember to be as specific as possible in describing the assets. You can include both solely owned assets and jointly owned assets in this section.

6. Print your name in the execution block on the last page and sign your name directly opposite the execution block in the space provided. You should sign your name in the presence of a witness. The witness should print and sign his/her name in the spaces provided under your execution block. You should repeat the process for your spouse.

Notice of Revocation

1. On the cover page, insert the date of execution of the notice of revocation as well as your name as grantor in the spaces provided.

2. On page 1, enter your name and address, the date the trust was established and the date of execution of the notice of revocation. Sign your name as grantor in the space provided.

3. The final page of the agreement contains a notary affidavit. There is generally no requirement that you have a notary complete this affidavit. However, we recommend that you have it completed as it lessens the likelihood that your execution of the notice of revocation could be challenged by others. Simply bring the notice together with identification to a notary and he or she will be able to assist you with the rest.

4. The notice should be sent to all trustees of the trust (including you).

Appendix 3

Revocable Living Trust Agreements

Revocable Living Trust Agreement for an Individual

Downloadable Forms

Blank copies of this form can be downloaded from the EstateBee website. Simply login to your account or, if you don't have an account, you can create one for free.

www.estate-bee.com/login

Once logged in, go to your profile page and enter the code listed below in the 'Use Codes' tab:

LTASIN129LTB

Revocable Living Trust Agreement

Agreement made this ____ day of _____, 20____.

Between:

(1) _____ of _____(the "Grantor"); and

(2) _____ of _____(the "Trustee").

Whereas:

A.   The Grantor is the legal and beneficial owner of the property described in the Schedule attached hereto.

B.   The Grantor wishes to create a trust of certain property for his benefit and for the benefit of others, such property being described in the Schedule attached hereto and having been delivered this date to the Trustee of the trust created hereunder.

C.   The Grantor may wish to add other property to the trust at a later date by gift, devise or bequest under the terms of a Last Will and Testament or otherwise by depositing such other property with the Trustee (or with any Successor Trustee).

D.   The Trustee is willing and hereby agrees to perform the duties of trustee in accordance with the terms and conditions and within the powers and limitations set out in this Agreement.

It is Agreed as Follows:

In consideration of the mutual covenants set forth herein, and for other good and valuable consideration (receipt of which is hereby acknowledged), the Grantor and Trustee hereby agree as follows:

1.   **Name of The Trust**

1.1   This trust shall be designated as the _____ Revocable Living Trust (the "**Trust**").

2. **Transfer of Property**

2.1 The Grantor, in consideration of the acceptance by Trustee of the trust herein created, hereby conveys, transfers, assigns, and delivers to the Trustee the property described in the Schedule hereto (the "Trust Estate") to hold same on trust for the uses and purposes set out below and in accordance with the terms of this Agreement.

2.2 The Grantor, and any other persons, shall have the right at any time to add property acceptable to the Trustee to the Trust and such property, when received and accepted by the Trustee, shall become a part of the Trust Estate and shall be noted in the Schedule hereto.

2.3 Notwithstanding any other provision of this Agreement, if the Grantorï¿½s principal place of residence forms part of the Trust Estate, the Grantor hereby reserves the right to possess, occupy and enjoy such premises and its surrounds for life, rent-free and without charge save for any taxes and other expenses properly payable by the Grantor.

3. **Disposition of Income and Principal During the Life of the Grantor**

3.1 The Trustee shall manage, invest and hold the Trust Estate and collect the income derived therefrom and, after the payment of all taxes and assessments thereon and all charges incident to the management thereof, dispose of the net income therefrom and corpus thereof, as follows:

3.1.1 During the lifetime of Grantor, the Trustee shall pay the income arising to the Trust Estate, together with such portions of the principal as the Grantor may from time to time direct, to the Grantor or otherwise as the Grantor may from time to time direct during his life.

3.1.2 During the lifetime of the Grantor, the Trustee may pay to or apply for the benefit of the Grantor such sums from the principal of the Trust as the Trustee shall in his absolute discretion consider necessary or advisable from time to time for the medical care, comfortable maintenance and welfare of the Grantor, taking into consideration any other income or resources of the Grantor known to the Trustee.

3.1.3 The Grantor may at any time during his lifetime and from time to time, withdraw all or part of the principal of the Trust, free of trust, by delivering to the Trustee an instrument in writing duly signed by the Grantor describing the property or portion thereof to be withdrawn. Upon receipt of such instrument, the Trustee shall thereupon convey, assign, deliver and execute any document necessary and do every act or thing necessary to transfer to the Grantor, free from the provisions of this Trust, the property described in the said instrument.

3.1.4   In the event that the Grantor is deemed to be mentally incompetent (as determined in writing by a qualified medical doctor) and unable to manage his own affairs, or in the event that the Grantor is not adjudicated incompetent, but by reason of illness or mental or physical disability is, in the reasonable opinion of the Successor Trustee, unable to properly handle his own affairs, then and in that event the Successor Trustee may during the Grantor's lifetime, in addition to the payments of income and principal for the benefit of the Grantor (including the medical care, comfortable maintenance and welfare of the Grantor), pay to or apply for the benefit of the Grantor's minor children and other dependents (if any), such sums from the net income and from the principal of this Trust in such shares and proportions as the Successor Trustee determines to be necessary or advisable from time to time for the medical care, comfortable maintenance and welfare of the Grantor's minor children and dependents taking into consideration, to the extent the Successor Trustee deems fit, any other income or resources of the Grantor's minor children and dependents known to the Successor Trustee.

3.1.5   The interests of the Grantor shall at all times be considered primary and superior to the interests of any beneficiary hereunder.

4. Division and Distribution of Trust Estate Following the Death of the Grantor

4.1 After the death of the Grantor, the Successor Trustee shall promptly distribute the Trust Estate to the following persons (the "Beneficiaries") as follows:

4.1.1   _____ of _____ shall be given _____ _____.

4.1.2   _____ of _____ shall be given _____ _____.

[Repeat or delete as necessary to make further specific gifts. Note you may need to renumber subsequent clauses]

4.1.3   Any of the Trust Estate not otherwise disposed of hereunder (the "Residue Trust Estate") shall be given to _____ of _____ for his/her own use and benefit absolutely. If the aforementioned person predeceases the Grantor then, in that event, his/her share of the Residue Trust Estate shall be given to _____ of _____.

5.   Property Management

5.1   The Successor Trustee shall be entitled (but shall not be obliged) to transfer the share of any minor Beneficiary for whom alternative property management provisions have not otherwise been made herein to the legal guardian or custodian of the Beneficiary upon production of such evidence by the said guardian or custodian to establish to the reasonable satisfaction of the Successor Trustee that such person stands as legal guardian or custodian to the said Beneficiary. Any such transfer shall be a good discharge of the Successor Trustee's obligations in that respect.

6.   Powers of Trustees

6.1   In addition to any powers granted under applicable law or otherwise, and not in limitation of such powers, but subject to any rights and powers which may be reserved expressly by the Grantor in this Agreement, the Trustee and any Successor Trustee validly acting hereunder (each a "trustee") shall have full power:

6.1.1   to hold and retain any and all property, real, personal, or mixed, received from any other source for such time as the trustee shall deem fit, and to dispose of such property by sale, exchange, assignment, lease, license or otherwise, as and when they shall deem fit;

6.1.2   to sell, assign, exchange, transfer, partition, convey, license, lease, rent, hire, grant options over or otherwise dispose of any property, real or personal, which forms part of the Trust Estate, upon such terms and conditions and in such manner as the trustee deems fit; and for that purpose to make, execute, acknowledge and deliver any and all instruments, deeds and assignments in such form and with such warranties and covenants as the trustee may deem fit;

6.1.3   to lease, license, rent and manage any or all of the assets, real or personal, of the Trust Estate, upon such terms and conditions as the trustee in his/her absolute discretion deems fit; and for that purpose to make, execute, acknowledge and deliver any and all instruments, deeds and assignments in such form and with such warranties and covenants as the trustee may deems fit; and to make repairs, replacements, and improvements, structural and otherwise, to any property, and to charge the expense thereof in an equitable manner to the principal or income of the Trust Estate, as the trustee deems fit;

6.1.4   to borrow money for any purpose in connection with the Trust, and to execute promissory notes or other obligations for amounts so borrowed, and to secure the payment of any such amounts by mortgage or pledge or any real or personal property, and to renew or extend the time of payment of any obligation, secured or unsecured, payable to or by any trust created hereby, for such periods of time as the trustee may deem fit;

6.1.5   to invest any or all of the funds of the Trust Estate in such manner as the trustee, acting in his/her absolute discretion, deems fit;

6.1.6   to deal with the Trust Estate generally for the benefit of the Beneficiaries;

6.1.7   to compromise, adjust, arbitrate, sue, institute, defend, abandon, settle or otherwise deal with proceedings of any kind on behalf of or against the Trust or the Trust Estate as the trustee shall in his/her sole and absolute discretion deem fit;

6.1.8   to determine in a fair and reasonable manner whether any part of the Trust Estate, or any addition or increment thereto be income or principal, or whether any cost, charge, expense, tax, or assessment shall be charged against income or principal, or partially against income and partially against principal;

6.1.9   to vote any stock, shares, bonds, securities or any other voting rights held by the Trust or attributable to the Trust Estate; and to delegate such voting power in such manner as the trustee may deem fit having regard to any legal requirements;

6.1.10   to consent to the reorganization, consolidation, merger, liquidation, readjustment of, or other change in any corporation, company, or association and to execute such documents and do all such acts and things as may reasonably be required to effect same;

6.1.11   to engage in business with the Trust Estate property as sole proprietor, or as a general or limited partner, with all the powers customarily exercised by an individual so engaged in business, and to hold an undivided interest in any property as tenant in common or as tenant in partnership, to the extent permitted by law; and to enter into such agreements and contracts as the trustee may deem necessary to regulate such businesses;

6.1.12   to purchase securities, real estate, or other property from any party connected to the Grantor, be it by contract or blood, provided such purchase is on an arm's length basis at market value and same is in the best interest of the Grantor and the Beneficiaries hereunder;

6.1.13   to make loans or advancements (secured or unsecured) to any party connected to the Grantor, be it by contract or blood, provided such loans or advancements are on an arm's length basis and in the best interest of the Grantors and the Beneficiaries hereunder;

6.1.14   to act through an agent or attorney-in-fact, by and under a power of attorney duly executed by the trustee to the extent permitted by law, in carrying out any of the authorized powers and duties; and

6.1.15   to undertake such further acts as are incidental to any of the foregoing or are reasonably required to carry out the tenor, purpose, and intent of the Trust.

6.2   The powers granted to the Trustee and Successor Trustee under Clause 6.1 may be exercised in whole or in part, from time to time, and shall be deemed to be supplementary to and not exclusive of the general powers of trustees pursuant to law, and shall include all powers necessary to carry them into effect.

6.3   Notwithstanding anything contained herein to the contrary, no powers enumerated or accorded to trustees generally pursuant to law shall be construed to enable the Grantor, or the Trustee or either of them, or any other person, to sell, purchase, exchange, or otherwise deal with or dispose of all or any part of the corpus or income of the trusts for less than an adequate consideration in money or money's worth, or to enable the Grantor to borrow all or any part of the corpus or income of the trusts, directly or indirectly, without adequate interest or security.

7. Successor Trustee

7.1 In the event of the death or during any period of incapacity of the Trustee, _____ of _____ is hereby nominated and appointed as the successor trustee to the trustee (the "Successor Trustee"). In the event the aforementioned person is unable or unwilling to act as Successor Trustee, _____ of _____ is hereby nominated and appointed as Successor Trustee.

7.2 If none of the persons named in Clause 7.1 are able and willing to act as successor trustee, then any of the nominated Successor Trustees may appoint a replacement successor trustee to serve as Successor Trustee hereunder provided that such appointment is made in writing, signed by the Successor Trustee making the appointment, notarized and forwarded to each of the named Beneficiaries. In the event the that no Successor Trustee is willing and able to make such an appointment or in the event that the Successor Trustee fails to secure the appointment of a new Successor Trustee and notify the Beneficiaries of such appointment within 7 days of the declining Successor Trustee's written refusal to act, then the next Successor Trustees shall be chosen by a majority in interest of the then living Beneficiaries, with a parent or guardian voting for each minor Beneficiary.

7.3 On acting, a Successor Trustee may, by notice in writing to the next Successor Trustee or to all Beneficiaries, resign from office at any time provided at least 14 days' notice in writing of such resignation is provided. The resigning Successor Trustee shall prior to his or her resignation taking effect deliver an accounting of the assets, income, and expenses of the Trust (and all sub-trusts, if any) to the next Successor Trustee. This accounting shall be made up to the date of resignation of the Successor Trustee. In the event of there being no readily identifiable Successor Trustee, the resigning Successor Trustee shall procure the appointment of a new Successor Trustee which may for the avoidance of doubt include a bank or trust company and shall notify the Beneficiaries in writing in the manner described in Clause 7.2 above. In the event that the Successor Trustee fails to secure the appointment of a new Successor Trustee and notify the Beneficiaries of same before the date of his or her resignation taking effect, then the next Successor Trustee shall be chosen by a majority in interest of the then living Beneficiaries, with a parent or guardian voting for each minor Beneficiary.

7.4 The appointment of the Successor Trustee(s) under this Clause shall automatically terminate at the end of any period in which the Grantor is incapacitated but such termination shall not impact the automatic re-appointment of such Successor Trustee(s) on the death of the Grantor or during any period of future incapacity of the Grantor, as contemplated by Clause 7.1.

7.5 A Successor Trustee shall (in his/her capacity as Successor Trustee) be able to exercise all the powers of the Trustee hereunder including, for the avoidance of doubt, but not limited to, the powers of the Trustee referred to in Clauses 3 to 6 hereof.

7.6 The Trustee and each Successor Trustee named herein (including any alternate named herein) shall serve without bond. A resigning Successor Trustee may require a bond to be posted by any other incoming Successor Trustee, the cost of such bond being payable from the Trust Estate. The Successor Trustee shall not be liable for any mistake or error of judgment in the administration of the Trust, except for willful misconduct, so long as they continue to exercise their duties and powers in a fiduciary capacity primarily in the interests of the Beneficiaries.

8. Revocation and Amendment

8.1 Subject The Grantor shall have the irrevocable right to and may by instrument in writing signed by the Grantor and delivered to the Trustee, revoke, modify or alter this Agreement, in whole or in part, without the consent of the Trustee or any Beneficiary. Save as may otherwise be provided herein, the Trust shall not be amended, modified, revoked, or terminated in any other way.

9. Administrative Provisions

9.1 The Trustee may at his absolute discretion, but shall not be obliged to, render an accounting at any time.

9.2 The Trustee hereby waives the payment of any compensation for his services, but this waiver shall not apply to any Successor Trustee who qualifies and acts under this Agreement and who shall be entitled to reasonable compensation for his or her service.

9.3 This Trust has been accepted by the Trustee and will be administered in the State of _____ and its validity, construction, and all rights hereunder shall be governed by the laws of that State and that State shall have exclusive jurisdiction to determine any disputes which may arise hereunder.

In **Witness Whereof,** the Grantor and Trustee have executed this Agreement on the date above written.

_____
Signature of Grantor

_____
Signature of Trustee

_____
Name of First Witness   _____
                                         Signature of First Witness

_____
Name of Second Witness   _____
                                         Signature of Second Witness

Schedule

Trust Property

_____
_____
_____
_____
_____
_____
_____
_____
_____
_____
_____
_____
_____
_____
_____
_____

_____

_____

_____

_____

_____

_____

_____

_____

_____

_____

_____

_____

_____

_____

_____

_____

_____

_____

_____

_____

_____

_____

_____

_____

_____

_____

Notary Affidavit

State of _____   County of _____

On _____ before me, _____, a notary public, personally appeared _____ who proved to me on the basis of satisfactory evidence to be the person whose name is subscribed to the within instrument and acknowledged to me that he/she executed the same in his/her authorized capacities, and that by his/her signature on the instrument he/she executed the instrument. I certify under PENALTY OF PERJURY that the foregoing is true and correct.

Witness my hand and official seal.

Signature: _____

Print Name: _____

My commission expires on: _____

(Seal)

Revocable Living Trust Agreement for a Couple

Downloadable Forms

Blank copies of this form can be downloaded from the EstateBee website. Simply login to your account or, if you don't have an account, you can create one for free.

www.estate-bee.com/login

Once logged in, go to your profile page and enter the code listed below in the 'Use Codes' tab:

LTAMAR129LTB

Revocable Living Trust Agreement

Agreement made this _____ day of _____, 20 ___.

Between:

(1) _____ of _____ ("First Grantor") and ____
_____ of _____ ("Second Grantor") in their capacity
as grantors of the Trust (the "Grantors"); and

(2) The First Grantor and the Second Grantor in their capacity as trustees of the Trust (the "Trustees").

Whereas:

A. The First Grantor is the legal and beneficial owner of the property described in Schedule One attached hereto.

B. The Second Grantor is the legal and beneficial owner of the property described in Schedule Two attached hereto.

C. The First Grantor and the Second Grantor jointly own the property described in Schedule Three.

D. The Grantors wish to create a trust of certain property for the benefit of themselves and others, such property being described in Schedules One, Two and Three attached hereto and having been delivered this date to the Trustees of the trust created hereunder.

E. The Grantors may wish to add other property to the trust at a later date by gift, devise or bequest under the terms of a Last Will and Testament or otherwise by depositing such other property with the Trustees (or with any Successor Trustee).

F. The Trustees are willing and hereby agree to perform the duties of trustee in accordance with the terms and conditions and within the powers and limitations set out in this Agreement.

It is Agreed as Follows:

In consideration of the mutual covenants set forth herein, and for other good and valuable consideration (receipt of which is hereby acknowledged), the Grantors and Trustees hereby agree as follows:

1. Name of The Trust

1.1 This trust shall be designated as the _____ Revocable Living Trust (the **"Trust"**).

2. Transfer of Property

2.1 The Grantors, in consideration of the acceptance by Trustees of the trust herein created, hereby jointly and severally convey, transfer, assign, and deliver to the Trustees the property described in Schedules One, Two and Three hereto (the "Trust Estate") to hold same on trust for the uses and purposes set out below and in accordance with the terms of this Agreement.

2.2 The Grantors, and any other persons, shall have the right at any time to add property acceptable to the Trustees to the Trust and such property, when received and accepted by the Trustees, shall become a part of the Trust Estate and shall be held in accordance with the terms of this Agreement, in particular Clause 2.4, and shall be noted accordingly in the relevant Schedule hereto.

2.3 Notwithstanding any other provision of this Agreement, if the Grantors' principal place of residence forms part of the Trust Estate, the Grantors hereby reserve the right to possess, occupy and enjoy such premises and its surrounds for life without fee or charge save that they shall be accountable for any taxes and other expenses properly payable by them in respect of such property.

2.4 For so long as both Grantors remain alive:

2.4.1 The First Grantor shall retain all control of and rights to all income and profits derived from the assets of the Trust Estate described in Schedule One;

2.4.2 The Second Grantor shall retain all control of and rights to all income and profits derived from the assets of the Trust Estate described in Schedule Two; and

2.4.3 The First Grantor and the Second Grantor shall respectively retain all control over and all rights to income and profits derived from their respective assets of the Trust Estate described in Schedule Three.

3. Disposition of Income and Principal During the Life of the Grantors

3.1 The Trustees shall manage, invest and hold the Trust Estate and collect the income derived therefrom and, after the payment of all taxes and assessments thereon and all charges incident to the management thereof, dispose of the net income therefrom and corpus thereof, as follows:

    3.1.1   For so long as both Grantors shall be living, the Trustees shall pay to:

    (a) First Grantor (or as he or she may otherwise direct) the income arising to that part of the Trust Estate described in Schedule One, together with such portions of the related principal as he or she may from time to time direct;

    (b) Second Grantor (or as he or she may otherwise direct) the income arising to that part of the Trust Estate described in Schedule Two, together with such portions of the related principal as he or she may from time to time direct; and

    (c) the Grantors (jointly) (or as they may otherwise jointly direct in writing) the income arising to that part of the Trust Estate described in Schedule Three, together with such portions of the related principal as they may from time to time direct in writing.

    3.1.2   During the lifetime of the Grantors, the Trustees may pay to or apply for the benefit of the Grantors such sums from the principal of the Trust as the Trustees shall in their absolute discretion consider necessary or advisable from time to time for the medical care, comfortable maintenance and welfare of the Grantors, taking into consideration any other income or resources of the Grantors known to the Trustees.

    3.1.3

    (a) First Grantor may at any time withdraw all or part of the principal of the

Trust Estate described in Schedule One (free of trust) by delivering to the Trustees an instrument in writing duly signed by him.

(b) Second Grantor may at any time withdraw all or part of the principal of the Trust Estate described in Schedule Two (free of trust) by delivering to the Trustees an instrument in writing duly signed by her.

(c) The Grantors, acting jointly, may at any time withdraw all or part of the principal of the Trust Estate described in Schedule Three (free of trust) by delivering to the Trustees an instrument in writing duly signed by each of them. Upon receipt of such instrument, the Trustees shall thereupon convey, assign, deliver and execute any document necessary and do every act or thing necessary to transfer to the Grantors, or either of them as the case may be, free from the provisions of this Trust, the property described in the said instrument.

3.1.4   In the event that both the Grantors are deemed to be mentally incompetent (as determined in writing by a qualified medical doctor) and unable to manage their own affairs, or in the event that the Grantors are not adjudicated incompetent, but by reason of illness or mental or physical disability are, in the reasonable opinion of the Successor Trustee, unable to properly handle their own affairs, then and in that event the Successor Trustee may during the Grantors' lifetimes, in addition to the payments of income and principal for the benefit of the Grantors, pay to or apply for the benefit of the Grantors' minor children and other dependents (if any), such sums from the net income and from the principal of this Trust in such shares and proportions as the Successor Trustee shall determine to be necessary or advisable from time to time for the medical care, comfortable maintenance and welfare of the Grantors' minor children and dependents taking into consideration, to the extent the Successor Trustee deems fit, any other income or resources of the Grantors' minor children and dependents known to the Successor Trustee.

3.1.5   The interests of the Grantors shall at all times be considered primary and superior to the interests of any beneficiary hereunder.

4.   Division and Distribution of Trust Estate Following the Death of a Grantor

4.1 Immediately upon the death of a Grantor (the "Deceased Grantor"), the Trust shall hereby be deemed to automatically divide into two separate trusts, to be known as the First Trust and the Second Trust, each of which is to be governed in the manner set out herein and the Surviving Grantor shall serve as trustee of each such trust.

4.2   Subject to Clause 4.3, the First Trust shall be deemed to and shall hereby include (i) all the Trust Estate owned by the Deceased Grantor immediately prior to its transfer to the Trust (ii) together with an amount in monitory value equal to the Deceased Grantor's share of the Trust Estate described in Schedule Three as at the date of death of the Deceased Grantor (iii) plus any related accumulated income, appreciation in value or assets represented thereby or derived therefrom and attributable to the ownership by the Deceased Grantor of the Trust Estate. The remainder of the Trust Estate shall vest in the Second Trust.

4.3   Any property of the Trust Estate gifted by the Deceased Grantor to the Surviving Grantor shall remain in the Second Trust.

4.4   The First Trust shall be irrevocable from inception. The Second Trust shall be revocable from inception but shall become irrevocable on the death of the Surviving Grantor.

4.5   Save in respect of any gifts made by the Deceased Grantor to the Surviving Grantor, the surviving Trustee shall distribute the property contained in the First Trust in accordance with the provisions of Clause 4.6 below.

4.6

4.6.1   On the death of First Grantor, the Trust Estate described in Schedule One and First Grantor's share of the Trust Estate described in Schedule Three shall be promptly distributed to the following persons (the "Beneficiaries") as follows:

(a)   _____ of _____ shall be given _____
         _____.

(b)   _____ of _____ shall be given _____
         _____.

[Repeat or delete as necessary to make further specific gifts. Note you may need to renumber subsequent clauses]

(c)   _____ of _____ shall be given First
        Grantor's interest in _____.

(d)   _____ of _____ shall be given First
        Grantor's interest in _____.

[Repeat or delete as necessary to make further specific gifts. Note you may need to renumber subsequent clauses]

(e)   Any of First Grantor's Trust Estate not otherwise disposed of hereunder
        ("First Grantor's Residue Trust Estate") shall be given to _____
        of _____ for his/her own use and benefit absolutely.
        If the aforementioned person predeceases the First Grantor or refuses the
        gift, then in that event his/her share of First Grantor's Residue Trust Estate
        shall be given to _____ of _____.

4.6.2   On the death of Second Grantor, the Trust Estate described in Schedule One and
        Second Grantor's share of the Trust Estate described in Schedule Three shall be
        promptly distributed to the following persons (also the "Beneficiaries") as follows:

(a)   _____ of _____ shall be given _____
        _____.

(b)   _____ of _____ shall be given _____
        _____.

[Repeat or delete as necessary to make further specific gifts. Note you may need to renumber subsequent clauses]

(c)   _____ of _____ shall be given Second
        Grantor's interest in _____.

(d)   _____ of _____ shall be given Second
        Grantor's interest in _____.

[Repeat or delete as necessary to make further specific gifts. Note you may need to renumber subsequent clauses]

(e)   Any of Second Grantor's Trust Estate not otherwise disposed of hereunder ("Second Grantor's Residue Trust Estate") shall be given to _____ of _____ for his/her own use and benefit absolutely. If the aforementioned person predeceases the Second Grantor then in that event his/her share of Second Grantor's Residue Trust Estate shall be given to _____ of _____.

4.7   If both Grantors die in circumstances which make it difficult or impossible to determine who predeceased the other, then for the purpose of this Agreement it shall be conclusively presumed that both died at the same moment and that neither survived the other. In such circumstances, the Successor Trustee shall distribute the Trust Estate in accordance with the wishes of each Grantor as described in Clause 4.6 above.

5.   Property Management

5.1   The Successor Trustee shall be entitled (but shall not be obliged) to transfer the share of any minor Beneficiary for whom alternative property management provisions have not otherwise been made herein to the legal guardian or custodian of the Beneficiary upon production of such evidence by the said guardian or custodian to establish to the reasonable satisfaction of the Successor Trustee that such person stands as legal guardian or custodian to the said Beneficiary. Any such transfer shall be a good discharge of the Successor Trustee's obligations in that respect.

6.   Administration of The Second Trust

6.1   The Second Trust shall be administered for the benefit of the Surviving Grantor in the manner described at Clause 3 above and the Trustee of the Second Trust shall have all of the rights referred to therein as well as any other rights of Trustees hereunder.

6.2   Upon the death of the Surviving Grantor, the Trust property contained in the Second Trust shall be distributed to the beneficiaries of the Surviving Grantor in the manner set out in Clause 4.6 above.

7.   Powers of Trustees

7.1 In addition to any powers granted under applicable law or otherwise, and not in limitation of such powers, but subject to any rights and powers which may be reserved expressly by the Grantors in this Agreement, the Trustees appointed hereunder shall have full power:

    7.1.1   to hold and retain any and all property, real, personal, or mixed, received from any other source for such time as the Trustees shall deem fit, and to dispose of such property by sale, exchange, assignment, lease, license or otherwise, as and when they shall deem fit;

    7.1.2   to sell, assign, exchange, transfer, partition, convey, license, lease, rent, hire, grant options over or otherwise dispose of any property, real or personal, which forms part of the Trust Estate, upon such terms and conditions and in such manner as the Trustees deem fit; and for that purpose to make, execute, acknowledge and deliver any and all instruments, deeds and assignments in such form and with such warranties and covenants as the Trustees may deem fit;

    7.1.3   to lease, license, rent and manage any or all of the assets, real or personal, of the Trust Estate, upon such terms and conditions as the Trustees in their absolute discretion deem fit; and for that purpose to make, execute, acknowledge and deliver any and all instruments, deeds and assignments in such form and with such warranties and covenants as the Trustees may deem fit; and to make repairs, replacements, and improvements, structural and otherwise, to any property, and to charge the expense thereof in an equitable manner to the principal or income of the Trust Estate, as the Trustees deem fit;

    7.1.4   to borrow money for any purpose in connection with the Trust, and to execute promissory notes or other obligations for amounts so borrowed, and to secure the payment of any such amounts by mortgage or pledge or any real or personal property, and to renew or extend the time of payment of any obligation, secured or unsecured, payable to or by any trust created hereby, for such periods of time as the Trustees may deem fit;

    7.1.5   to invest any or all of the funds of the Trust Estate in such manner as the Trustees, acting in their absolute discretion, deem fit;

    7.1.6   to deal with the Trust Estate generally for the benefit of the Beneficiaries;

7.1.7   to compromise, adjust, arbitrate, sue, institute, defend, abandon, settle or otherwise deal with proceedings of any kind on behalf of or against the Trust or the Trust Estate as the Trustees shall in their sole and absolute discretion deem fit;

7.1.8   to determine in a fair and reasonable manner whether any part of the Trust Estate, or any addition or increment thereto be income or principal, or whether any cost, charge, expense, tax, or assessment shall be charged against income or principal, or partially against income and partially against principal;

7.1.9   to engage and compensate agents, accountants, brokers, attorneys-in-fact, attorneys-at-law, tax specialists, realtors, custodians, investment counsel, and other assistants and advisors, and to do so without liability for any neglect, omission, misconduct, or default of any such agent or professional representative, provided he or she was selected and retained with reasonable care;

7.1.10   to vote any stock, shares, bonds, securities or any other voting rights held by the Trust or attributable to the Trust Estate; and to delegate such voting power in such manner as the Trustees may deem fit having regard to any legal requirements;

7.1.11   to consent to the reorganization, consolidation, merger, liquidation, readjustment of, or other change in any corporation, company, or association and to execute such documents and do all such acts and things as may reasonably be required to effect same;

7.1.12   to engage in business with the Trust Estate property as sole proprietor, or as a general or limited partner, with all the powers customarily exercised by an individual so engaged in business, and to hold an undivided interest in any property as tenant in common or as tenant in partnership, to the extent permitted by law; and to enter into such agreements and contracts as the Trustee(s) may deem necessary to regulate such businesses;

7.1.13   to purchase securities, real estate, or other property from any party connected to the Grantors (or either of them), be it by contract or blood, provided such purchase is on an arm's length basis at market value and same is in the best interest of the Grantors and the Beneficiaries hereunder;

7.1.14   to make loans or advancements (secured or unsecured) to any party connected to the Grantors (or either of them), be it by contract or blood, provided such loans and advancements are on an arm's length basis at market value and same are in the best interest of the Grantors and the Beneficiaries hereunder;

7.1.15   to act through an agent or attorney-in-fact, by and under a power of attorney duly executed by the Trustees to the extent permitted by law, in carrying out any of the authorized powers and duties; and

7.1.16   to undertake such further acts as are incidental to any of the foregoing or are reasonably required to carry out the tenor, purpose and intent of the Trust.

7.2   The powers granted to the Trustees and Successor Trustee under Clause 8.1 may be exercised in whole or in part, from time to time, and shall be deemed to be supplementary to and not exclusive of the general powers of trustees pursuant to law, and shall include all powers necessary to carry them into effect.

7.3   Notwithstanding anything contained herein to the contrary, no powers enumerated or accorded to trustees generally pursuant to law shall be construed to enable the Grantors, or the Trustees or either of them, or any other person, to sell, purchase, exchange, or otherwise deal with or dispose of all or any part of the corpus or income of the trusts for less than an adequate consideration in money or money's worth, or to enable the Grantors to borrow all or any part of the corpus or income of the trusts, directly or indirectly, without adequate interest or security.

8.   Successor Trustee

8.1   On the death of or during any period of disability of either of the Grantors, the other Grantor shall serve as sole Trustee. In the event of the death or during any period of incapacity of both Grantors, _____ of _____ shall be appointed as Successor Trustee. In the event the aforementioned person is unable or unwilling to act as Successor Trustee, _____ of _____ shall serve as Successor Trustee.

8.2   If none of the persons named in Clause 8.1 are able and willing to act as successor trustee, then any nominated Successor Trustee may appoint a replacement successor trustee to serve as Successor Trustee hereunder provided that such appointment is made in writing, signed by the Successor Trustee making the appointment, notarized and forwarded to each of the named Beneficiaries. In the event that no Successor Trustee is willing and able to make such an appointment or in the event that the Successor Trustees fail to secure the appointment of a new Successor Trustee and notify the Beneficiaries of such appointment within 7 days of the declining Successor Trustee's written refusal to act, then the next Successor Trustee shall be chosen by a majority in interest of the then living Beneficiaries, with a parent or guardian voting for each minor Beneficiary.

8.3   On acting, a Successor Trustee may, by notice in writing to the next Successor Trustee or to all Beneficiaries, resign from office at any time provided at least 14 days' notice in writing of such resignation is provided. The resigning Successor Trustee shall prior to his or her resignation taking effect deliver an accounting of the assets, income, and expenses of the Trust (and all sub-trusts, if any) to the next Successor Trustee. This accounting shall be made up to the date of resignation of the Successor Trustee. In the event of there being no readily identifiable Successor Trustee, the resigning Successor Trustee shall procure the appointment of a new Successor Trustee which may for the avoidance of doubt include a bank or trust company and shall notify the Beneficiaries in writing in the manner described in Clause 8.2 above. In the event that the Successor Trustee fails to secure the appointment of a new Successor Trustee and notify the Beneficiaries of same before the date of his or her resignation taking effect, then the next Successor Trustee shall be chosen by a majority in interest of the then living Beneficiaries, with a parent or guardian voting for each minor Beneficiary.

8.4   The appointment of the Successor Trustee under this Clause shall automatically terminate at the end of any period in which both Grantors were incapacitated but such termination shall not impact the automatic re-appointment of such Successor Trustee on the death of the Grantors or during any period of future incapacity of both Grantors, as contemplated by Clause 9.1.

8.5   A Successor Trustee shall (when validly acting in his/her capacity as successor trustee) be able to exercise all the powers of the Trustees hereunder including, for the avoidance of doubt, but not limited to, the powers of the Trustees referred to in Clause 3 to Clause 7 hereof as if he or she were a Trustee.

8.6   Trustees, Successor Trustee(s) and their successors shall serve without bond. The Successor Trustees shall not be liable for any mistake or error of judgment in the administration of the Trust, except for willful misconduct, so long as they continue to exercise their duties and powers in a fiduciary capacity primarily in the interests of the Beneficiaries.

9.   Revocation and Amendment

9.1 Subject to Clause 4.4, the Grantors, or the survivor of them, shall acting jointly (or alone in the case of the Surviving Grantor) have the right and may by instrument in writing signed by each of the Grantors, or the survivor of them as the case may be, and delivered to the Trustees, modify or alter this Agreement, in whole or in part, without the consent of the Trustees, any beneficiary or any other party.

9.2 Subject to Clause 4.4, either of the Grantors, or the survivor of them, shall have the right and may by instrument in writing signed by either of them, or the survivor of them as the case may be, and delivered to the Trustees and the other Grantor, revoke this Agreement in whole without the consent of the other Grantor, the Trustees or any beneficiary.

9.3 Save as may otherwise be provided herein, the Trust shall not be amended, modified, revoked, or terminated in any other way.

9.4 If the Trust is revoked, the Trustees shall promptly distribute the Trust Estate to the Grantors in such manner as would, as near as possible, restore the ownership of the Trust Estate to the manner in which it was held immediately prior to the transfer of the Trust Estate to the Trust.

10. Administrative Provisions

10.1 The Trustees may at their absolute discretion, but shall not be obliged to, render an accounting at any time.

10.2 The Trustees waive the payment of any compensation for their services, but this waiver shall not apply to any Successor Trustee who qualifies and acts under this Agreement and who shall be entitled to reasonable compensation for his or her service.

10.3 This Trust has been accepted by the Trustees and will be administered in the State of _____ and its validity, construction, and all rights hereunder shall be governed by the laws of that State and that State shall have exclusive jurisdiction to determine any disputes which may arise hereunder.

In Witness Whereof, the Grantors and Trustees have executed this Agreement on the date above written.

_____

Signature of Grantor

_____

Signature of Co-Grantor

_____

Signature of Trustee

_____

Signature of Co-Trustee

_____

Name of First Witness

_____

Signature of First Witness

_____

Name of Second Witness

_____

Signature of Second Witness

Schedule One
First Grantor's Trust Property

_____
_____
_____
_____
_____
_____
_____
_____
_____
_____
_____
_____
_____
_____
_____
_____
_____
_____
_____
_____
_____
_____
_____
_____
_____
_____
_____
_____
_____
_____
_____
_____
_____
_____
_____
_____
_____
_____
_____
_____

Schedule Two
Second Grantor's Trust Property

_____
_____
_____
_____
_____
_____
_____
_____
_____
_____
_____
_____
_____
_____
_____
_____
_____
_____
_____
_____
_____
_____
_____
_____
_____
_____
_____
_____
_____
_____
_____

Schedule Three
Jointly Held Property

_____

_____

_____

_____

_____

_____

_____

_____

_____

_____

_____

_____

_____

_____

_____

_____

_____

_____

_____

_____

_____

_____

_____

_____

_____

_____

_____

_____

_____

_____

_____

_____

_____

_____

_____

_____

_____

_____

Notary Affidavit

State of _____   **County of** _____

On _____ before me, _____, a notary public, personally appeared __
_____ and _____, who proved to me on the basis of
satisfactory evidence to be the persons whose names are subscribed to the within instrument and
acknowledged to me that they executed the same in their authorized capacities, and that by their
signatures on the instrument the persons executed the instrument. I certify under PENALTY OF
PERJURY that the foregoing is true and correct.

Witness my hand and official seal.

Signature: _____

Print Name: _____

My commission expires on: _____

(Seal)

AB Revocable Living Trust Agreement for a Couple

Downloadable Forms

Blank copies of this form can be downloaded from the EstateBee website. Simply login to your account or, if you don't have an account, you can create one for free.

www.estate-bee.com/login

Once logged in, go to your profile page and enter the code listed below in the 'Use Codes' tab:

LTAAB129LTB

AB Revocable Living Trust Agreement

Agreement made this _____ day of _____, 20_____.

Between:

(1) _____ of _____ ("**First Grantor**") and _____ _____ of _____ ("**Second Grantor**") in their capacity as grantors of the Trust (the "**Grantors**"); and

(2) The First Grantor and the Second Grantor in their capacity as trustees of the Trust (the "**Trustees**").

Whereas:

A. The First Grantor is the legal and beneficial owner of the property described in Schedule One attached hereto.

B. The Second Grantor is the legal and beneficial owner of the property described in Schedule Two attached hereto.

C. The First Grantor and the Second Grantor jointly own the property described in Schedule Three.

D. The Grantors wish to create a trust of certain property for the benefit of themselves and others, such property being described in Schedules One, Two and Three attached hereto and having been delivered this date to the Trustees of the trust created hereunder.

E. The Grantors may wish to add other property to the trust at a later date by gift, devise or bequest under the terms of a Last Will and Testament or otherwise by depositing such other property with the Trustees (or with any Successor Trustee).

F. The Trustees are willing and hereby agree to perform the duties of trustee in accordance with the terms and conditions and within the powers and limitations set out in this Agreement.

It is Agreed as Follows:

In consideration of the mutual covenants set forth herein, and for other good and valuable consideration (receipt of which is hereby acknowledged), the Grantors and Trustees hereby agree as follows:

1. Name of The Trust

1.1 This trust shall be designated as the _____ Revocable Living Trust (the "**Trust**").

2. Transfer of Property

2.1 The Grantors, in consideration of the acceptance by Trustees of the trust herein created, hereby jointly and severally convey, transfer, assign, and deliver to the Trustees the property described in Schedules One, Two and Three hereto (the "Trust Estate") to hold same on trust for the uses and purposes set out below and in accordance with the terms of this Agreement.

2.2 The Grantors, and any other persons, shall have the right at any time to add property acceptable to the Trustees to the Trust and such property, when received and accepted by the Trustees, shall become a part of the Trust Estate and shall be held in accordance with the terms of this Agreement, in particular Clause 2.4, and shall be noted accordingly in the relevant Schedule hereto.

2.3 Notwithstanding any other provision of this Agreement, if the Grantors' principal place of residence forms part of the Trust Estate, the Grantors hereby reserve the right to possess, occupy and enjoy such premises and its surrounds for life without fee or charge save that they shall be accountable for any taxes and other expenses properly payable by them in respect of such property.

2.4 For so long as both Grantors remain alive:

    2.4.1 The First Grantor shall retain all control of and rights to all income and profits derived from the assets of the Trust Estate described in Schedule One;

    2.4.2 The Second Grantor shall retain all control of and rights to all income and profits derived from the assets of the Trust Estate described in Schedule Two; and

    2.4.3 The First Grantor and the Second Grantor shall respectively retain all control over and all rights to income and profits derived from their respective assets of the Trust Estate described in Schedule Three.

3. Disposition of Income and Principal During the Life of the Grantors

3.1 The Trustees shall manage, invest and hold the Trust Estate and collect the income derived therefrom and, after the payment of all taxes and assessments thereon and all charges incident to the management thereof, dispose of the net income therefrom and corpus thereof, as follows:

    3.1.1   For so long as both Grantors shall be living, the Trustees shall pay to:

        (a)   First Grantor (or as he or she may otherwise direct) the income arising to that part of the Trust Estate described in Schedule One, together with such portions of the related principal as he or she may from time to time direct;

        (b)   Second Grantor (or as he or she may otherwise direct) the income arising to that part of the Trust Estate described in Schedule Two, together with such portions of the related principal as he or she may from time to time direct; and

        (c)   the Grantors (jointly) (or as they may otherwise jointly direct in writing) the income arising to that part of the Trust Estate described in Schedule Three, together with such portions of the related principal as they may from time to time direct in writing.

    3.1.2   During the lifetime of the Grantors, the Trustees may pay to or apply for the benefit of the Grantors such sums from the principal of the Trust as the Trustees shall in their absolute discretion consider necessary or advisable from time to time for the medical care, comfortable maintenance and welfare of the Grantors, taking into consideration any other income or resources of the Grantors known to the Trustees.

    3.1.3

        (a)   First Grantor may at any time withdraw all or part of the principal of the

Trust Estate described in Schedule One (free of trust) by delivering to the Trustees an instrument in writing duly signed by him.

(b) Second Grantor may at any time withdraw all or part of the principal of the Trust Estate described in Schedule Two (free of trust) by delivering to the Trustees an instrument in writing duly signed by her.

(c) The Grantors, acting jointly, may at any time withdraw all or part of the principal of the Trust Estate described in Schedule Three (free of trust) by delivering to the Trustees an instrument in writing duly signed by each of them. Upon receipt of such instrument, the Trustees shall thereupon convey, assign, deliver and execute any document necessary and do every act or thing necessary to transfer to the Grantors, or either of them as the case may be, free from the provisions of this Trust, the property described in the said instrument.

3.1.4   In the event that both the Grantors are deemed to be mentally incompetent (as determined in writing by a qualified medical doctor) and unable to manage their own affairs, or in the event that the Grantors are not adjudicated incompetent, but by reason of illness or mental or physical disability are, in the reasonable opinion of the Successor Trustee, unable to properly handle their own affairs, then and in that event the Successor Trustee may during the Grantors' lifetimes, in addition to the payments of income and principal for the benefit of the Grantors, pay to or apply for the benefit of the Grantors' minor children and other dependents (if any), such sums from the net income and from the principal of this Trust in such shares and proportions as the Successor Trustee shall determine to be necessary or advisable from time to time for the medical care, comfortable maintenance and welfare of the Grantors' minor children and dependents taking into consideration, to the extent the Successor Trustee deems fit, any other income or resources of the Grantors' minor children and dependents known to the Successor Trustee.

3.1.5   The interests of the Grantors shall at all times be considered primary and superior to the interests of any beneficiary hereunder.

4.   Division and Distribution of Trust Estate Following the Death of a Grantor

4.1 Immediately upon the death of a Grantor (the "Deceased Grantor"), the Trust shall hereby be deemed to automatically divide into two separate trusts, to be known as the First Trust and the Second Trust, each of which is to be governed in the manner set out herein and the Surviving Grantor shall serve as trustee of each such trust.

4.2 Subject to Clause 4.3, the First Trust shall be deemed to and shall hereby include (i) all the Trust Estate owned by the Deceased Grantor immediately prior to its transfer to the Trust (ii) together with an amount in monitory value equal to the Deceased Grantor's share of the Trust Estate described in Schedule Three as at the date of death of the Deceased Grantor (iii) plus any related accumulated income, appreciation in value or assets represented thereby or derived therefrom and attributable to the ownership by the Deceased Grantor of the Trust Estate. The remainder of the Trust Estate shall vest in the Second Trust.

4.3 Any property of the Trust Estate gifted by the Deceased Grantor to the Surviving Grantor shall remain in the Second Trust.

4.4 The First Trust shall be irrevocable from inception. The Second Trust shall be revocable from inception but shall become irrevocable on the death of the Surviving Grantor.

4.5 Save in respect of any gifts made by the Deceased Grantor to the Surviving Grantor, the surviving Trustee shall distribute the property contained in the First Trust in accordance with the provisions of Clause 4.6 below.

4.6

4.6.1 On the death of First Grantor, the Trust Estate described in Schedule One and First Grantor's share of the Trust Estate described in Schedule Three shall be promptly distributed to the following persons (the "**Beneficiaries**") as follows:

(a) _____ of _____ shall be given _____ _____.

(b) _____ of _____ shall be given _____ _____.

[Repeat or delete as necessary to make further specific gifts. Note you may need to renumber subsequent clauses]

(c) _____ of _____ shall be given First Grantor's interest in _____.

(d) _____ of _____ shall be given First Grantor's interest in _____.

[Repeat or delete as necessary to make further specific gifts. Note you may need to renumber subsequent clauses]

(e) Any of First Grantor's Trust Estate not otherwise disposed of hereunder (**"First Grantor's Residue Trust Estate"**) shall be given to the Second Grantor for life provided he or she survives the First Grantor and thereafter to _____ of _____ for his/her own use and benefit absolutely. If the aforementioned person predeceases the Second Grantor then in that event his/her share of First Grantor's Residue Trust Estate shall be given to _____ of _____.

4.6.2 On the death of Second Grantor, the Trust Estate described in Schedule One and Second Grantor's share of the Trust Estate described in Schedule Three shall be promptly distributed to the following persons (the "**Beneficiaries**") as follows:

(a) _____ of _____ shall be given _____ _____.

(b) _____ of _____ shall be given _____ _____.

[Repeat or delete as necessary to make further specific gifts. Note you may need to renumber subsequent clauses]

(c) _____ of _____ shall be given Second Grantor's interest in _____.

(d) _____ of _____ shall be given Second Grantor's interest in _____.

[Repeat or delete as necessary to make further specific gifts. Note you may need to renumber subsequent clauses]

(e)   Any of Second Grantor's Trust Estate not otherwise disposed of hereunder (**"Second Grantor's Residue Trust Estate"**) shall be given to First Grantor for life provided he or she survives the Second Grantor and thereafter to _____ of _____ for his/her own use and benefit absolutely. If the aforementioned person predeceases the First Grantor then in that event his/her share of Second Grantor's Residue Trust Estate shall be given to _____ of _____.

4.7 If both Grantors die in circumstances which make it difficult or impossible to determine who predeceased the other, then for the purpose of this Agreement it shall be conclusively presumed that both died at the same moment and that neither survived the other. In such circumstances, the Successor Trustee shall distribute the Trust Estate in accordance with the wishes of each Grantor as described in Clause 4.6 above.

5.   Property Management

5.1 The Successor Trustee shall be entitled (but shall not be obliged) to transfer the share of any minor Beneficiary for whom alternative property management provisions have not otherwise been made herein to the legal guardian or custodian of the Beneficiary upon production of such evidence by the said guardian or custodian to establish to the reasonable satisfaction of the Successor Trustee that such person stands as legal guardian or custodian to the said Beneficiary. Any such transfer shall be a good discharge of the Successor Trustee's obligations in that respect.

6.   Administration of the First Trust

6.1 The First Trust shall (unless otherwise instructed by the Surviving Grantor) be administered for the benefit of the Surviving Grantor (who will have a life interest in that trust) and for the ultimate beneficiaries of the residual interest in that First Trust (as described above).

6.2 The Trustee shall, on a quarterly annual basis, pay to or spend for the benefit of the Surviving Grantor the net income of the First Trust.

6.3 During the lifetime of the Surviving Grantor, the Trustee shall pay to or apply for the benefit of the Surviving Grantor such sums from the principal of the First Trust as the Trustee shall in his/her absolute discretion consider necessary or advisable from time to time for the medical care, comfortable maintenance, education and welfare of the Surviving Grantor, taking into consideration any other income or resources of the Surviving Grantor known to the Trustee.

6.4 Upon the death of the Surviving Grantor, the Trust Estate contained in the First Trust shall be distributed to the beneficiaries of the Deceased Grantor's residual element of the Trust Estate as described in Clause 4.6 above.

6.5 The Trustee shall not be obliged to prepare accounts in respect of the First Trust save that the residual beneficiaries shall be provided with copies of the annual federal income tax return in respect of the First Trust.

6.6 The Trustee shall be entitled to reasonable and appropriate compensation from the assets of the First Trust for administration services rendered in respect of that trust.

7. Administration of The Second Trust

7.1 The Second Trust shall be administered for the benefit of the Surviving Grantor in the manner described at Clause 3 above and the Trustee of the Second Trust shall have all of the rights referred to therein as well as any other rights of Trustees hereunder.

7.2 Upon the death of the Surviving Grantor, the Trust property contained in the Second Trust shall be distributed to the beneficiaries of the Surviving Grantor in the manner set out in Clause 4.6 above.

8. Powers of Trustees

8.1 In addition to any powers granted under applicable law or otherwise, and not in limitation of such powers, but subject to any rights and powers which may be reserved expressly by the Grantors in this Agreement, the Trustees appointed hereunder shall have full power:

8.1.1 to hold and retain any and all property, real, personal, or mixed, received from any other source for such time as the Trustees shall deem fit, and to dispose of such property by sale, exchange, assignment, lease, license or otherwise, as and when they shall deem fit;

8.1.2   to sell, assign, exchange, transfer, partition, convey, license, lease, rent, hire, grant options over or otherwise dispose of any property, real or personal, which forms part of the Trust Estate, upon such terms and conditions and in such manner as the Trustees deem fit; and for that purpose to make, execute, acknowledge and deliver any and all instruments, deeds and assignments in such form and with such warranties and covenants as the Trustees may deem fit;

8.1.3   to lease, license, rent and manage any or all of the assets, real or personal, of the Trust Estate, upon such terms and conditions as the Trustees in their absolute discretion deem fit; and for that purpose to make, execute, acknowledge and deliver any and all instruments, deeds and assignments in such form and with such warranties and covenants as the Trustees may deem fit; and to make repairs, replacements, and improvements, structural and otherwise, to any property, and to charge the expense thereof in an equitable manner to the principal or income of the Trust Estate, as the Trustees deem fit;

8.1.4   to borrow money for any purpose in connection with the Trust, and to execute promissory notes or other obligations for amounts so borrowed, and to secure the payment of any such amounts by mortgage or pledge or any real or personal property, and to renew or extend the time of payment of any obligation, secured or unsecured, payable to or by any trust created hereby, for such periods of time as the Trustees may deem fit;

8.1.5   to invest any or all of the funds of the Trust Estate in such manner as the Trustees, acting in their absolute discretion, deem fit;

8.1.6   to deal with the Trust Estate generally for the benefit of the Beneficiaries;

8.1.7   to compromise, adjust, arbitrate, sue, institute, defend, abandon, settle or otherwise deal with proceedings of any kind on behalf of or against the Trust or the Trust Estate as the Trustees shall in their sole and absolute discretion deem fit;

8.1.8   to determine in a fair and reasonable manner whether any part of the Trust Estate, or any addition or increment thereto be income or principal, or whether any cost, charge, expense, tax, or assessment shall be charged against income or principal, or partially against income and partially against principal;

8.1.9   to engage and compensate agents, accountants, brokers, attorneys-in-fact, attorneys-at-law, tax specialists, realtors, custodians, investment counsel, and other assistants and advisors, and to do so without liability for any neglect, omission, misconduct, or default of any such agent or professional representative, provided he or she was selected and retained with reasonable care;

8.1.10   to vote any stock, shares, bonds, securities or any other voting rights held by the Trust or attributable to the Trust Estate; and to delegate such voting power in such manner as the Trustees may deem fit having regard to any legal requirements;

8.1.11   to consent to the reorganization, consolidation, merger, liquidation, readjustment of, or other change in any corporation, company, or association and to execute such documents and do all such acts and things as may reasonably be required to effect same;

8.1.12   to engage in business with the Trust Estate property as sole proprietor, or as a general or limited partner, with all the powers customarily exercised by an individual so engaged in business, and to hold an undivided interest in any property as tenant in common or as tenant in partnership, to the extent permitted by law; and to enter into such agreements and contracts as the Trustee(s) may deem necessary to regulate such businesses;

8.1.13   to purchase securities, real estate, or other property from any party connected to the Grantors (or either of them), be it by contract or blood, provided such purchase is on an arm's length basis at market value and same is in the best interest of the Grantors and the Beneficiaries hereunder;

8.1.14   to make loans or advancements (secured or unsecured) to any party connected to the Grantors (or either of them), be it by contract or blood, provided such loans and advancements are on an arm's length basis at market value and same are in the best interest of the Grantors and the Beneficiaries hereunder;

8.1.15   to act through an agent or attorney-in-fact, by and under a power of attorney duly executed by the Trustees to the extent permitted by law, in carrying out any of the authorized powers and duties; and

8.1.16   to undertake such further acts as are incidental to any of the foregoing or are reasonably required to carry out the tenor, purpose and intent of the Trust.

8.2   The powers granted to the Trustees and Successor Trustee under Clause 8.1 may be exercised in whole or in part, from time to time, and shall be deemed to be supplementary to and not exclusive of the general powers of trustees pursuant to law, and shall include all powers necessary to carry them into effect.

8.3   Notwithstanding anything contained herein to the contrary, no powers enumerated or accorded to trustees generally pursuant to law shall be construed to enable the Grantors, or the Trustees or either of them, or any other person, to sell, purchase, exchange, or otherwise deal with or dispose of all or any part of the corpus or income of the trusts for less than an adequate consideration in money or money's worth, or to enable the Grantors to borrow all or any part of the corpus or income of the trusts, directly or indirectly, without adequate interest or security.

9.   Successor Trustee

9.1   On the death of or during any period of disability of either of the Grantors, the other Grantor shall serve as sole Trustee. In the event of the death or during any period of incapacity of both Grantors, _____ of _____ shall be appointed as Successor Trustee. In the event the aforementioned person is unable or unwilling to act as Successor Trustee, _____ of _____ shall serve as Successor Trustee.

9.2   If none of the persons named in Clause 9.1 are able and willing to act as successor trustee, then any nominated Successor Trustee may appoint a replacement successor trustee to serve as Successor Trustee hereunder provided that such appointment is made in writing, signed by the Successor Trustee making the appointment, notarized and forwarded to each of the named Beneficiaries. In the event that no Successor Trustee is willing and able to make such an appointment or in the event that the Successor Trustees fail to secure the appointment of a new Successor Trustee and notify the Beneficiaries of such appointment within 7 days of the declining Successor Trustee's written refusal to act, then the next Successor Trustee shall be chosen by a majority in interest of the then living Beneficiaries, with a parent or guardian voting for each minor Beneficiary.

9.3   On acting, a Successor Trustee may, by notice in writing to the next Successor Trustee or to all Beneficiaries, resign from office at any time provided at least 14 days' notice in writing of such resignation is provided. The resigning Successor Trustee shall prior to his or her resignation taking effect deliver an accounting of the assets, income, and expenses of the Trust (and all sub-trusts, if any) to the next Successor Trustee. This accounting shall be made up to the date of resignation of the Successor Trustee. In the event of there being no readily identifiable Successor Trustee, the resigning Successor Trustee shall procure the appointment of a new Successor Trustee which may for the avoidance of doubt include a bank or trust company and shall notify the Beneficiaries in writing in the manner described in Clause 9.2 above. In the event that the Successor Trustee fails to secure the appointment of a new Successor Trustee and notify the Beneficiaries of same before the date of his or her resignation taking effect, then the next Successor Trustee shall be chosen by a majority in interest of the then living Beneficiaries, with a parent or guardian voting for each minor Beneficiary.

9.4 The appointment of the Successor Trustee under this Clause shall automatically terminate at the end of any period in which both Grantors were incapacitated but such termination shall not impact the automatic re-appointment of such Successor Trustee on the death of the Grantors or during any period of future incapacity of both Grantors, as contemplated by Clause 9.1.

9.5 A Successor Trustee shall (when validly acting in his/her capacity as successor trustee) be able to exercise all the powers of the Trustees hereunder including, for the avoidance of doubt, but not limited to, the powers of the Trustees referred to in Clause 3 to Clause 8 hereof as if he or she were a Trustee.

9.6 Trustees, Successor Trustee(s) and their successors shall serve without bond. The Successor Trustees shall not be liable for any mistake or error of judgment in the administration of the Trust, except for willful misconduct, so long as they continue to exercise their duties and powers in a fiduciary capacity primarily in the interests of the Beneficiaries.

10. Revocation and Amendment

10.1 Subject to Clause 4.4, the Grantors, or the survivor of them, shall acting jointly (or alone in the case of the Surviving Grantor) have the right and may by instrument in writing signed by each of the Grantors, or the survivor of them as the case may be, and delivered to the Trustees, modify or alter this Agreement, in whole or in part, without the consent of the Trustees, any beneficiary or any other party.

10.2 Subject to Clause 4.4, either of the Grantors, or the survivor of them, shall have the right and may by instrument in writing signed by either of them, or the survivor of them as the case may be, and delivered to the Trustees and the other Grantor, revoke this Agreement in whole without the consent of the other Grantor, the Trustees or any beneficiary.

10.3 Save as may otherwise be provided herein, the Trust shall not be amended, modified, revoked, or terminated in any other way.

10.4 If the Trust is revoked, the Trustees shall promptly distribute the Trust Estate to the Grantors in such manner as would, as near as possible, restore the ownership of the Trust Estate to the manner in which it was held immediately prior to the transfer of the Trust Estate to the Trust.

11. Administrative Provisions

11.1 The Trustees may at their absolute discretion, but shall not be obliged to, render an accounting at any time.

11.2 The Trustees waive the payment of any compensation for their services, but this waiver shall not apply to any Successor Trustee who qualifies and acts under this Agreement and who shall be entitled to reasonable compensation for his or her service.

11.3 This Trust has been accepted by the Trustees and will be administered in the State of _____ _____ and its validity, construction, and all rights hereunder shall be governed by the laws of that State and that State shall have exclusive jurisdiction to determine any disputes which may arise hereunder.

In Witness Whereof, the Grantors and Trustees have executed this Agreement on the date above written.

_____
Signature of Grantor

_____
Signature of Co-Grantor

_____
Signature of Trustee

_____
Signature of Co-Trustee

_____   _____
Name of First Witness   Signature of First Witness

_____   _____
Name of Second Witness   Signature of Second Witness

Schedule One
First Grantor's Trust Property

_____
_____
_____
_____
_____
_____
_____
_____
_____
_____
_____
_____
_____
_____
_____
_____
_____
_____
_____
_____
_____
_____
_____
_____
_____
_____
_____
_____
_____
_____
_____
_____
_____
_____
_____
_____
_____
_____
_____

Schedule Two
Second Grantor's Trust Property

_____
_____
_____
_____
_____
_____
_____
_____
_____
_____
_____
_____
_____
_____
_____
_____
_____
_____
_____
_____
_____
_____
_____
_____
_____
_____
_____
_____
_____
_____
_____
_____
_____
_____
_____
_____
_____
_____

Schedule Three
Jointly Held Property

_____
_____
_____
_____
_____
_____
_____
_____
_____
_____
_____
_____
_____
_____
_____
_____
_____
_____
_____
_____
_____
_____
_____
_____
_____
_____
_____
_____
_____
_____
_____
_____
_____

Notary Affidavit

State of _____   County of _____

On _____ before me, _____, a notary public, personally appeared _____ and _____, who proved to me on the basis of satisfactory evidence to be the persons whose names are subscribed to the within instrument and acknowledged to me that they executed the same in their authorized capacities, and that by their signatures on the instrument the persons executed the instrument. I certify under PENALTY OF PERJURY that the foregoing is true and correct.

Witness my hand and official seal.

Signature: _____

Print Name: _____

My commission expires on: _____

(Seal)

Appendix 4

Miscellaneous Clauses for Use in a Revocable Living Trust Agreement

Downloadable Forms

Blank copies of this form can be downloaded from the EstateBee website. Simply login to your account or, if you don't have an account, you can create one for free.

www.estate-bee.com/login

Once logged in, go to your profile page and enter the code listed below in the 'Use Codes' tab:

MISC129LTB

Additional Clauses That You May Wish to Add

Custodianship Under UTMA

This clause should be placed in the property management section if required.

1.1   All property left under the terms of this revocable living trust to _____
shall be given to _____ of _____, in the capacity
of custodian of _____ under the _____ Uniform
Transfers to Minors Act, to hold until _____ reaches 21 years of age. If the
aforementioned person is unwilling or unable to serve as custodian for any reason, then
_____ of _____ shall be hereby appointed as custodian
instead.

Child's Sub-Trust for Living Trust

This clause should be placed in the property management section if required.

1.1.1 In the event that _____ has not reached the age of _____ years
on the date of [Grantor Name]'s death, then any property left to him/her under this revocable
living trust shall be retained in a sub-trust and held, managed and distributed for his/her
benefit. The sub-trust shall be known as the _____ sub-trust. The Successor
Trustee shall be trustee of this sub-trust. The sub-trust shall be managed by the Successor
Trustee in accordance with the provisions below.

1.1.2 So much of the income from an individual sub-trust and, if the net income be at any time
insufficient, so much of the principal of this sub-trust as may be deemed necessary in the
sole discretion of the Successor Trustee (taking into account all other sources of income,
support and circumstances of the sub-trust beneficiary of which the Successor Trustee
has knowledge) may be either paid to or expended on behalf of the sub-trust beneficiary
(whichever in the Successor Trustee's sole discretion is deemed most appropriate) in order
to ensure the support, maintenance, health, and education (including collegiate, vocational,
professional, etc.) of the sub-trust beneficiary.

1.1.3 A sub-trust shall terminate on the earliest to occur of the following:

(i)   when the sub-trust beneficiary reaches the age set out in the clause establishing
that sub-trust beneficiary's sub-trust above, in which case the principal, together

with any accumulations of income of the sub-trust, shall be paid over and distributed to the said sub-trust beneficiary; or

(ii)   the sub-trust principal is exhausted through distributions validly made under the sub-trust provisions herein; or

(iii)   on the death of the sub-trust beneficiary, in which case the property being held for that trust beneficiary shall be paid over and distributed (i) under the terms of the sub-trust beneficiary's Will, (ii) to the sub-trust beneficiary's issue (if any), per stirpes, or in default of such, (iii) to the sub-trust beneficiary's brothers and sisters and descendants of deceased brothers and sisters, per stirpes, or, in default of such,(iv) to the Grantor's heirs, determined as if he had died at the time of the sub-trust beneficiary's death pursuant to the General Statutes of _____ _____.

1.2 No interest hereunder shall be transferable or assignable by any Beneficiary, or be subject during his or her life to the claims of his or her creditors.

1.3 Notwithstanding anything herein to the contrary, the trusts created under this Clause shall terminate not later than twenty-one (21) years after the death of the last Beneficiary named herein.

Appointment of Alternate Beneficiary of a Specific Gift

Below are sample clauses used to nominate alternate beneficiaries for specific gifts under a revocable living trust.

Single Trust

_____ of _____ shall be given _____ . If the aforementioned person does not survive the Grantor the said property shall be given to _____ of _____ .

Shared or Couple's Trust

_____ of _____ shall be given _____. If the aforementioned person does not survive _____ the said property shall be given to _____ of _____.

Gift of Residue to More than One Person – Single Trust

The clause below is a sample clause that can be used to distribute the residuary trust estate amongst more than one person. The successor trustee will be responsible for dividing the residuary trust estate in the percentages specified.

In sub-clause (i) below, one alternate beneficiary is appointed.

In sub-clause (ii) below, a number of alternates are appointed and each will receive a specified percent of the primary beneficiary's estate if the primary beneficiary fails to survive the grantor.

You can decide how many alternates you wish to nominate (if any) for each primary beneficiary and use the appropriate clause.

4.1.1   Any of the Trust Estate not otherwise disposed of hereunder (the "Residue Trust Estate") shall be divided by the Successor Trustee as follows:

(i)   _____% thereof shall be given to _____ of _____ _____. In the event that the aforementioned person shall fail to survive the Grantor, his/her share of the Residue Trust Estate shall be given to _____ of _____.for his/her own use and benefit absolutely.

(ii)   _____% thereof shall be given to _____ of _____ _____. In the event that the aforementioned person shall fail to survive the Grantor, his/her share of the Residue Trust Estate shall be divided by the Successor Trustee as follows:

i   _____% thereof shall be given to _____ of _____ _____.

ii   _____% thereof shall be given to _____ of _____ _____.

Gift of Residue to More than One Person – Shared or Couple's Trust

4.1.1   Any of _____'s Trust Estate not otherwise disposed of hereunder ("_____'s Residue Trust Estate") shall be divided by the Successor Trustee as follows:

(i)   _____% thereof shall be given to _____ of _____ _____. In the event that the aforementioned person shall fail to survive the Grantor, his/her share of the Residue Trust Estate shall be given to _____ of _____.for his/her own use and benefit absolutely.

(ii)   _____% thereof shall be given to _____ of _____ _____. In the event that the aforementioned person shall fail to survive the Grantor, his/her share of the Residue Trust Estate shall be divided by the Successor Trustee as follows:

i   _____% thereof shall be given to _____ of _____ _____.

ii   _____% thereof shall be given to _____ of _____ _____.

Appendix 5

Deed of Assignment

Deed of Assignment for Use with An Individual Revocable Living Trust

Deed of Assignment

This Deed is made on this _____ day of _____, 20 ___.

Between:

(1) _____ of _____ in his/her capacity as grantor of
   the Trust (the "Grantor"); and

(2) _____ of _____ in his/her capacity as trustee of
   the Trust (the "**Trustee**").

Whereas:

A. Pursuant to a Revocable Living Trust Agreement dated day of 20___, made between the
   Grantor and the Trustee, the Grantor created a trust known as _____(the
   "Trust").

B. The Grantor is the legal and beneficial owner of the property described in Clause 1 below (the
   "**Property**").

C. The Grantor has agreed to assign all of the Grantor's rights, interests and entitlements in the
   Property to the Trust and the Trustee has agreed to accept such assignment subject to the
   terms and conditions of this Deed.

1.   Assignment of Property

1.1 For good and valuable consideration (the receipt of which is hereby acknowledged), the
   Grantor hereby absolutely and unconditionally assigns all the Grantor's rights, entitlements,
   interests in and to the following property:

   _____
   _____
   _____
   _____

   -to the Trustee, as trustee of the Trust.

2.   Binding on Successors

2.1 This Deed shall be binding upon and ensure to the benefit of the respective parties hereto and their respective personal representatives and successors.

3.   Notice

3.1 Any notice or other communication given or made under this Deed shall be in writing and shall be delivered to the relevant party or sent by first class mail to the address of that party specified in this Deed or to such other address as may be notified hereunder by that party from time to time for this purpose.

3.2 Unless the contrary shall be proved, each such notice or communication shall be deemed to have been given, made and delivered, if by letter, 48 hours after posting or if by delivery, when left at the relevant address.

4.   Counterparts

4.1 This Deed may be executed in any number of counterparts and by the different parties hereto on separate counterparts each of which when executed and delivered shall constitute an original and all such counterparts together constituting but one and the same instrument.

5.   Severability

5.1 Each of the provisions of this Deed is separate and severable and enforceable accordingly and if at any time any provision is adjudged by any court of competent jurisdiction to be void or unenforceable the validity, legality and enforceability of the remaining provisions hereof and of that provision in any other jurisdiction shall not in any way be affected or impaired thereby.

6.   Whole Agreement

6.1 This Deed contains the whole agreement between the parties hereto relating to the matters provided for in this Deed and supersedes all previous deeds or agreements (if any) between such parties in respect of such matters and each of the parties to this Deed acknowledges that in agreeing to enter into this Deed it has not relied on any representations or warranties except for those contained in this Deed.

As Witness the parties hereto have executed this document as a deed on the date appearing at the head hereof.

Executed and Delivered as a Deed

By _____ (print name)

As Grantor and Trustee

_____

(Signature)

In the presence of:

_____

(Name of witness)

_____

(Signature)

Deed of Assignment for Use With
A Couple's Revocable Living Trust

Downloadable Forms

Blank copies of this form can be downloaded from the EstateBee website. Simply login to your account or, if you don't have an account, you can create one for free.

www.estate-bee.com/login

Once logged in, go to your profile page and enter the code listed below in the 'Use Codes' tab:

Assignment129LTB

Deed of Assignment

This Deed is made on this _____ day of _____, 20_____.

Between:

(1) _____ of _____ and _____
of _____ in their capacity as grantors of the Trust (the
"Grantors"); and

(2) _____ of _____ and _____
of _____ in their capacity as trustees of the Trust (the "Trustees").

Whereas:

A. Pursuant to a Revocable Living Trust Agreement dated day of 20___, made between the
Grantors and the Trustees, the Grantors created a trust known as _____
_____(the "Trust").

B. The Grantors (or either of them) are the legal and beneficial owners of the property described
in Clause 1 below (the "Property").

C. The Grantors have agreed to assign all of their respective rights, interests and entitlements in
the Property to the Trust and the Trustees have agreed to accept such assignment subject to
the terms and conditions of this Deed.

1.   Assignment of Property

1.1 For good and valuable consideration (the receipt of which is hereby acknowledged), the
Grantors hereby absolutely and unconditionally assign all of their respective rights,
entitlements, interests in and to the following property:

_____
_____
_____
_____
_____
_____

to the Trustees, as trustees of the Trust.

2.   Binding on Successors

2.1 This Deed shall be binding upon and ensure to the benefit of the respective parties hereto and their respective personal representatives and successors.

3. Notice

3.1 Any notice or other communication given or made under this Deed shall be in writing and shall be delivered to the relevant party or sent by first class mail to the address of that party specified in this Deed or to such other address as may be notified hereunder by that party from time to time for this purpose.

3.2 Unless the contrary shall be proved, each such notice or communication shall be deemed to have been given, made and delivered, if by letter, 48 hours after posting or if by delivery, when left at the relevant address.

4. Counterparts

4.1 This Deed may be executed in any number of counterparts and by the different parties hereto on separate counterparts each of which when executed and delivered shall constitute an original and all such counterparts together constituting but one and the same instrument.

5. Severability

5.1 Each of the provisions of this Deed is separate and severable and enforceable accordingly and if at any time any provision is adjudged by any court of competent jurisdiction to be void or unenforceable the validity, legality and enforceability of the remaining provisions hereof and of that provision in any other jurisdiction shall not in any way be affected or impaired thereby.

6. Whole Agreement

6.1 This Deed contains the whole agreement between the parties hereto relating to the matters provided for in this Deed and supersedes all previous deeds or agreements (if any) between such parties in respect of such matters and each of the parties to this Deed acknowledges that in agreeing to enter into this Deed it has not relied on any representations or warranties except for those contained in this Deed.

As Witness the parties hereto have executed this document as a deed on the date appearing at the head hereof.

Executed and Delivered as a Deed

By _____ (print name)

As Grantor and Trustee   _____
                                       (Signature)

In the presence of:

_____
(Name of witness)

_____
(Signature)

Executed and Delivered as a Deed

By _____ (print name)

As Grantor and Trustee   _____
                                       (Signature)

In the presence of:

_____
(Name of witness)

_____
(Signature)

Appendix 6

Notice of Revocation of a Living Trust

Downloadable Forms

Blank copies of this form can be downloaded from the EstateBee website. Simply login to your account or, if you don't have an account, you can create one for free.

www.estate-bee.com/login

Once logged in, go to your profile page and enter the code listed below in the 'Use Codes' tab:

Revocation129LTB

Notice of Revocation

I, _____ of _____, as grantor under a Revocable Living Trust Agreement dated the _____ day of _____, 20_____ (the "Agreement") wherein you are designated as a trustee, or have been appointed successor trustee thereunder, do hereby revoke the powers and trusts created and conferred by me under the terms of the Agreement.

I hereby direct you, as trustee, to turn over and deliver to me all property held by you subject to the terms and provisions of the Agreement and to which I am entitled following this revocation, together with all accumulations of interest and income and any rights to which I am or ought to be beneficially entitled.

This REVOCATION is made this the _____ day of _____, 20_____.

_____

Grantor

Notary Affidavit

State of _____   **County of** _____

On _____ before me, _____, a notary public, personally appeared _____, who proved to me on the basis of satisfactory evidence to be the person whose name is subscribed to the within instrument and acknowledged to me that he/she executed the same in his/her authorized capacity, and that by his/her signature on the instrument the person executed the instrument. I certify under penalty of perjury that the foregoing is true and correct

Witness my hand and official seal.

Signature _____

My Commission Expires:

_____

(SEAL)

EstateBee's Estate Planning Range

Make Your Own
Last Will & Testament

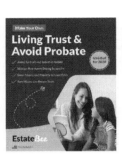

Make Your Own
Living Trust & Avoid
Probate

Make Your Own
Medical & Financial
Power of Attorney

How to Probate an
Estate - A Step-by-Step
Guide for Executors

Estate Planning
Essentials - A Step-by-
Step Guide to Estate
Planning

Funeral Planning Basics
– A Step-by-Step Guide
to Funeral Planning

Legal Will Kit

Living Trust Kit

Healthcare Power of
Attorney & Living
Will Kit

Codicil to a Last
Will & Testament Kit

Durable General
Power of Attorney Kit

Durable Limited
Power of Attorney Kit

EstateBee's Online Will Writer

Create Your Estate Planning Documents Online in Minutes...

EstateBee's online software enables you to create bespoke estate planning documents such as wills, living trusts, living wills and powers of attorney from the comfort of your own home.

The software uses documents which have been pre-approved by experienced estate planning lawyers and are tailored to comply with the individual laws of each state (except Louisiana).

Using a simple question and answer process, you'll be able to create a document which is bespoke to your individual circumstances. The process only takes a few minutes and help, and information are available at every step.

> **Get Started Online Now**

Why choose EstateBee's Online Will Writer

✓ Save Time and Money

✓ Created by Experienced Attorneys

✓ Advanced Features

✓ Compliant with US Laws

✓ Bank Level Encryption

✓ 20+ years in Business

Proud to have helped thousands of people make wills, trusts, and powers of attorney online over the past 20 years.

Estate*Bee*

About EstateBee

EstateBee, the internationally recognized publisher of estate planning products, was founded in 2000 by lawyers from one of the most prestigious international law firms in the world. Its aim was simple – to provide access to quality legal information and products at an affordable price.

Made in United States
Orlando, FL
15 December 2021

11850579R00137